ALSO BY JOSEPH LELYVELD

Move Your Shadow:
South Africa, Black and White

OMAHA BLUES

OMAHA BLUES

A MEMORY LOOP

JOSEPH LELYVELD

FARRAR, STRAUS AND GIROUX / NEW YORK

Farrar, Straus and Giroux
19 Union Square West, New York 10003

Copyright © 2005 by Joseph Lelyveld
Distributed in Canada by Douglas & McIntyre Ltd.
Printed in the United States of America
First edition, 2005

Library of Congress Cataloging-in-Publication Data
Lelyveld, Joseph.
    Omaha blues : a memory loop / Joseph Lelyveld.—1st ed.
      p.   cm.
    ISBN-13: 978-0-374-22590-2
    ISBN-10: 0-374-22590-7 (alk. paper)
    1. Lelyveld, Arthur J., 1913–   2. Rabbis—Ohio—Cleveland—Biography.
  3. Anti-communist movements—United States—History—20th century.
  4. Internal security—United States—History—20th century.   I. Title.

CT275.L (Lelyveld, Arthur) L (Lelyveld, Joseph) +

                                                        2004012362

Designed by Jonathan D. Lippincott

www.fsgbooks.com

1   3   5   7   9   10   8   6   4   2

These pages were for Carolyn, love of my life.

They are also for my brothers, David and Michael;
for the five grandchildren of Toby and Arthur Lelyveld—
Amy, Nita, Adam, Svati, and Victor—and for the first great-
grandchild, Alice Rose, who came into our lives, providentially,
after her birth in or near the Yangtze River town of Fuling.

My mind plunged away from me, and I suddenly found myself thinking of the places and people of my own infinitesimal past.

—Willa Cather, *My Ántonia*

CONTENTS

OMAHA BLUES

1

MEMORY BOY

Long before I taught myself to hold them at a safe distance, my parents called me "the memory boy." If once I knew what they meant by that, the memory boy has long since forgotten, shedding memories and the stories behind pet phrases as so much extra baggage. The tag may have had something to do with my inability to forget the lyric of any song I heard as a child. But what I think it really described was a knack for recalling names and the order in which things happened: where we went on those rare occasions we went anywhere as a family, who we saw, who came to see us, what they said, and our verdicts later on, for as a family we were judgmental to a very considerable fault.

Shedding was an acquired skill, a way of getting on with life, which was what you had to do, I later told myself, once you closed your mind to the possibilities of therapy. "Getting on with life" became a slogan of my inner monologues; a catchword or, as I'd now say, admitting to wordplay, a catch cry. Even then, the knack for recalling names and the order of things survived, so long as they had little to do with me. It came in handy on college exams. It came in handy telling the stories of others, which is what I eventually did for a living. I could recall obscure facts, make intuitive connections, ask the right questions. And I could always move on to the next assignment, the next story, as journalists do. Moving on became my

particular way of getting on with life, and even if I now acknowledge it as a form of psychic flight, it seemed a liberating, sometimes
thrilling, way to live.

So I wasn't touched or curious or anyway receptive when, three
decades after my parents' divorce, my octogenarian father sent me a
packet of love letters between him and my mother that he'd hidden
away. He thought his posterity might be interested in preserving them.
Not me, his eldest son. I knew instantly that I didn't want to handle
them or own them, let alone read them. So I disposed of them and
then, characteristically, disposed of the memory of how I'd disposed
of them. Maybe I gave them to my mother; it might have seemed the
honorable thing to do. I mention this close brush with family history
now only to describe a reflex and to show how unlike me it was, several
years later, to go scavenging in the basement of a Cleveland synagogue while my dad, its emeritus rabbi of great eminence, lay helpless in a nearby hospice, his speech and understanding already
extinguished by a brain tumor, leaving only his sweetness to mark
him as the man we knew while he faded out.

The foray in the basement wasn't my idea. I'd been sitting quietly with my dad in his hospice room on a Saturday morning; as
quietly as you could given the TV din pouring from the surrounding
rooms, a universal anodyne for the dying even more than the living in
our land. There was no look of recognition in his eyes, but when I
held his hand I felt the comforting pressure of his grip. More for my
sake than his, since the words didn't register, I'd tell him I loved him,
but that still left plenty of time for sour-sweet reflection on the paradox of this unfailingly loving father who was almost as consistently
beyond reach. In the thirty-one years of his second marriage, which
had now lasted slightly longer than the one that produced me and
my two brothers, I'd found myself alone with him, talking directly,
on only a few occasions at best (in truth, only one I could now
clearly recall) before he started to die and I began making my visits
to the hospice room.

Geography was partly to blame—for many of these years we were thousands of miles apart—but there was also the inevitable balancing he had to do between his two families. Understandably, he was protective of his wife, a vivacious but easily offended person, so conversation that tended to exclude her, especially conversation that dwelled on memories she didn't share, had to be avoided. Our meetings became performances; if they came off reasonably well, without hurt feelings, as they almost always did, I could expect a good review. But then in the previous twenty-seven years, the years since my birth, he had often been unavailable for reasons that were not dissimilar: my mother, a more complicated person than my dad, sometimes needed to be protected from her children.

Sitting in his hospice room near the end of my sixth decade and his life, I could pretty much count the number of times we had gone somewhere or done something together in the years of my boyhood: three camping trips, one doubleheader at Yankee Stadium, a few Columbia football games, seven or eight sets of tennis (until, finally, I managed not to blow a lead); a single family vacation on the Gulf Coast of Florida; the annual drives to deposit us at summer camp in Maine (and then to haul us back); a few times when I tagged along on his out-of-town speaking engagements; irregular visits to Shabbat services at a half dozen synagogues in Manhattan in the years he had no congregation of his own; and a test for a junior driving license that I had already failed by the time Dad, from the backseat, gently noted that I still had the parking brake on. "You've just gone through your third stop sign," I recall him saying, "so I don't think it will hurt your chances if I ask you to release it."

Reaching back to that spring, when I was sixteen, I could also count a more cherished car memory. My dad and I were returning from Boston in the new powder blue Mercury convertible he'd gone all the way to Nebraska a few weeks earlier to purchase at dealer's cost; the top was down, and in keeping with the then universal belief that nothing could be more healthful than full, direct sunshine, we were wearing only sunglasses above our waists. The way I now fondly recall it, we were two characters in a buddy film zipping along at close to eighty miles an hour until Dad was pulled over by a Connecticut state trooper who, scanning his license, spotted the clerical title. There wasn't a hint of irony in the trooper's voice when he said, "I see you're a man of the cloth." Cloth was scarcely in evidence but we were sent on our way with a caution and no ticket, only to repeat the encounter ten minutes later with a second trooper who also let us go after remarking, with the same sacerdotal figure of speech, that my dad was "a man of the cloth." Thereafter, every time we told the story, we'd wonder whether the two troopers ever had a chance to compare notes back at the barracks. In my mind, that drive down from Boston remained a farcical high point of our relationship.

Later, when I was gone from the nest and in the first year of my own marriage, there had been the fearful hours we passed together in a hospital corridor, from past midnight to dawn, waiting to see whether my mother might recover from what I learned, only then, was her third suicide attempt. Wearily and quietly, Dad spoke of his touch-and-go struggle over the seventeen years since the first one to sustain my mother and their marriage, wondering now whether the effort had been misguided. In despair, as she hovered between life and death down the hall, he even wondered whether we had the right to try to reverse the choice she'd made only a few hours before.

Taken altogether, is that a lot of closeness or a little? I have a friend who has no direct memory of a father killed in World War II. He might consider it a lot. At the moment, I was struck by how much more it might have been, by the opportunities I'd let slide. I wasn't consciously drawing up a balance sheet on our joint venture as father and son, but it was hard not to be aware that the hours I was now passing in the hospice room with what remained of him gave me an unusual dose—too late, of course—of a closeness I'd long missed without fully realizing it. This was family history too, and it was only now, as I was beginning to let down my defenses, that a visitor to his room that Saturday asked whether I knew about the camp trunk in the temple's basement full of his first family's—my family's—effects; a much larger archive, it turned out, than the one I'd earlier spurned.

The visitor, a devoted friend of my dad's, led the way. He had been on the synagogue's staff and still had a key that we used to enter through the back. It wasn't exactly a heist, but we carried it off as a clandestine operation. A small Saturday morning congregation was praying in a chapel near the main sanctuary as we made our way quietly to the basement. Never having lived in Cleveland, I'd probably been in the building where my dad had held forth for three decades fewer than twenty times, which was most of the times I'd been in synagogues in my adult life, and I hadn't set foot there for several years. For me, religion was always something my dad did, and I did, if I did it at all, mainly to please him. I was usually moved when I had the opportunity to hear and watch him, but mine was a filial rather than a religious response. I basked in the warmth of his devotions, not my own. Without him, the experience of communal prayer, the only kind I practiced, was at best a matter of heritage, vaguely soothing in its way; at worst a matter of creepy sociology, leaving me with a sense of myself as standing outside the circle, a mere observer—a feeling that carried an annoying trace of guilt over my inability to find compelling meaning in words I'd heard since I'd first heard words. I had never gone to services on my own impulse, and needless to say, I was not on a religious errand now.

I recognized the labels on the battered old trunk, which sat on a shelf at about the height of my shoulders. I had to stand on tiptoe to peer inside. On top was a framed watercolor, a quiet Jerusalem landscape, signed by the artist "To Toby and Arthur," that had hung in our living room long ago. With the dissolution of that union, it had lost its place on Dad's wall. I swiftly appropriated it and then dug deeper through mounds of clippings, report cards, speech notes, typed correspondence, and family mail—letters from three boys in summer camp over many years and letters between our parents, scores of them, in periods in which they were apart before long-distance phoning became easy and affordable. The encounter with the archive, the detritus of a family, wasn't at that moment Proustian. It was suffocating. I closed the lid sharply, meaning to stick the genie of reminiscence and helpless disappointment back in its box, and returned to my station at my dad's bedside. Nevertheless, after he died several weeks later, I arranged to have the contents of the old trunk shipped to my Hudson Valley house, where, after a rough sorting, I left them to molder for another six years.

I got back to them by a roundabout route. Having run to the edge of a mandatory retirement age for bosses at the only newspaper at which I'd ever worked, I found myself with only myself to order around. The first assignment I gave myself as a reborn writer was one I'd talked idly about all my adult life. It was to write about Ben, the closest adult friend of my boyhood, to delve into the life story of an all but forgotten man and find a way to tell it; to make myself, in that sense, his biographer. Ben had been born in what was called Indian Territory before it became part of the new state of Oklahoma. He talked about the great Oklahoma land rush as if he'd been part of it, although it was already history when he came into the world, and about Choctaws and Cherokees as if he'd grown up with them. He never explained how he became a rabbi but was happy to talk about how he gave it up, how he was run out of his first pulpit in Montgomery, Alabama, for refusing to take a vow of silence in the case of the Scottsboro boys, nine black youths charged with the rapes of two white women, a case that repeatedly went to trial in the thirties and was not finally resolved till the last "boys" in Alabama's prisons were approaching middle age; by that time it had long faded as the sensational issue that Communists and others had made it in northern cities and around the globe. In my imagination, incited by a scrapbook of clippings Ben kept in the lower right-hand drawer of his desk at the office overlooking Times Square, crosses were burning on Montgomery lawns as he fled, casting lurid shadows.

I knew that Ben had later found his way to Hollywood, where he made a new life, and that somewhere in that passage he left his family, acquired a new wife and a new name too. He had been Benjamin Goldstein. He became Ben Lowell. I knew that he had at least one daughter by his first wife and that she now rode horses somewhere in Pennsylvania. I knew that he hadn't seen her as often as he wanted, and that his inexplicable readiness to spend afternoons and evenings accompanying an eleven- (later twelve-) year-old sports fanatic to ballgames might have something to do with this gap in his life and the likelihood—alluded to slyly by my mom and gradually made apparent by the fact that we saw a lot of Ben and little of Mrs. Lowell—that his second marriage hadn't been going too well either.

I didn't know why he decided to leave Hollywood and become a rabbi again, working for my dad in the national headquarters of the Hillel Foundations, a movement that maintained centers for Jewish students on college campuses. And I didn't tell myself then what now seems obvious, that he had begun to assume a role in my life that my dad, who was often on the road like his traveling salesman father before him, was usually too absent or too busy or too preoccupied to fill. For a couple of years, Ben was the one adult in my life who seemed consistently and reliably available. We started going to games in the fall of 1948, a year the Yankees finished third behind the Indians and the Red Sox. We must have gone to several baseball and football games over a few months because I remember feeling virtuous when, as a concession and a break from our custom, I agreed that my brother David, then only seven, could accompany us that same autumn to a Columbia-Syracuse football game at Baker's Field at the northern end of Manhattan Island.

It was the last game of the season and the seniors who had

ended a previously indomitable Army's thirty-two-game winning streak the year before would not be returning. For decades to come, Columbia football would be a joke, but that year few human activities mattered more to me. Ben, who never pretended to be a fan, would listen with good-humored patience while I provided a precociously detailed briefing on Gene Rossides and Lou Kusserow, the Columbia stars whose dorm rooms I'd been dropping in on every so often for about a year on my way home from school.

Becoming a juvenile groupie of Columbia varsity teams had been, I now suppose, a desperate attempt on my part to nail down an identity and context for myself after a series of uprootings including a whole year when my parents were separated and I lived with grandparents. Columbia was consecrated ground in the family photograph albums I had pored over. It was the scene of my father's undergraduate triumphs, on which my mother would sometimes

dwell with markedly more enthusiasm than she had come to show for his achievements as a rabbi. He had become the first Jewish editor of the *Columbia Spectator* after the expulsion of an editor who had crusaded against the overemphasis on sports in an era in which Columbia actually made it to the Rose Bowl (look it up). My dad continued the crusade, unable to imagine that his young son would become a small barnacle on the sports establishment he was assailing. And that wasn't all; as an undergraduate, he also found time to make the freshman wrestling team; to play soccer, not then a varsity sport; to be the leader of the Glee Club, take small parts in plays, earn the Phi Beta Kappa key he always wore on his old-fashioned watch chain, and lead a dance band he called the Columbia Ramblers, featuring himself on a four-string banjo and vocals. Columbia was also where my parents met and fell in love and where my glamorous mother was now striving for a doctorate with a thesis on how the character of Shylock had been interpreted by great and lesser Shakespearean actors from the Elizabethans down through Edwin Booth and Henry Irving to John Gielgud.

Columbia's campus was only a couple of blocks from where we had finally settled after years in the heartland of America: first in Ohio, where my dad had studied to be a rabbi and had his first congregation, then in Nebraska. When I gained free admission to all home basketball games by walking in at the age of ten as a kind of mascot with the pint-sized playmaker Sherry Marshall, the bulky, high-scoring center Walt Budko, and the other players, I felt it was something like a hereditary right.

My school, by contrast, was foreign territory. P.S. 165 on the Upper West Side of Manhattan was my fourth school in four years when I washed up there in third grade as an immigrant from Omaha by way of Brooklyn. Some of my classmates were Spanish-speaking and ate spicy food in contrast to Velveeta, Bird's Eye frozen peas (served frozen), Del Monte fruit cup, and the pink custard known as Junket, gustatory high points in the bland regimen on which my family subsisted. Others were refugees from Europe, also learning a new language. In Omaha I'd been unusual because I was the only Jew in public school classes where we sang "Jesus Wants Me for a Sunbeam" and "Jesus Loves Me, This I Know." ("We're so pleased to have Joseph," my kindergarten teacher told my dad on parents' day. "We've always had one.") On West 108th Street I was unusual because I seemed relatively well off by the school's humble standards, living as I did on Riverside Drive, and even a little exotic because of my claim of having hailed from the heartland. At least a half dozen kids in my class came from the Caribbean. No one else, I could be sure, had been anywhere near Nebraska. Inevitably, Omaha faded fast as a real place in my memory, but I clung to it for years for purposes of self-definition. Emptied of all other content, the word "Omaha" came to have a private meaning for me. It meant I'm not really from this place, Manhattan.

Columbia was also about self-definition. But even if I'm right in thinking now that going to Baker's Field was a way of connecting to my dad's undergraduate legacy on my own terms, on the rare occasions I managed to nag my dad into taking me there I actually found it less satisfying than going with Ben. Dad, a crusader no longer, sang "Roar, Lion Roar" more loudly, it seemed to me, than any other alumnus in the old wooden stands, drowning out and finally silencing my quavering soprano. In his company, I got to participate in his nostalgia. In Ben's, I took the lead. I knew I had little to tell Dad about Columbia, that he wasn't really interested in my hard-won knowledge of the career and ambitions of the quarterback. If the question had been put, I would certainly have confirmed that my parents loved me, but I'd never felt as indulged as I did in Ben's company. He would actually react when I told him that Rossides was the one athlete who was always studying when I barged into his room, that he wanted to go to law school rather than the pros like the legendary Sid Luckman, who'd gone on from Columbia to quarterback the Chicago Bears. My impression is that I never stopped talking because when I picture Ben he's generally smiling and nodding, encouraging me to go on.

He was forty-six that fall, eleven years older than my dad and, at about five foot ten, several inches taller, a husky, broad-shouldered man with crinkly good looks and expressive blue eyes that didn't look away. He also had a small scar on his upper lip. That's not something I could have told you before I got four big files from the FBI on a Freedom of Information request, once I started gathering material a few years ago on my old friend, a half century after he suddenly disappeared from my life. He was removed by my dad, who fired him for speeches that followed the Communist line; or, to split hairs I loyally learned to split in the middle of my fourteenth year, Dad didn't fire him but rather accepted Ben's resignation, which was de-manded, I was told and easily persuaded, not because he publicly associated himself with the view that the United States was the ag-gressor in Korea but because he'd earlier been untruthful about his involvement in the Communist Party. Yes, witch-hunters belonging to an outfit called the American Jewish League Against Communism had been screaming for his scalp. But no, Dad's organization had not succumbed to them. It had reacted to a betrayal at the personal level, a betrayal by Ben.

Now I think I can actually remember that little scar on Ben's lip. If so, it's obviously what psychologists call "cued recall," a term I recently picked up from David Zipser, a classmate of mine in that autumn of 1950 and earlier who is now a neuroscientist making computer models of the way the neurons in our brains fire each other up in efforts of human consciousness such as the attempt to make sense of the memories that give form to our lives. You see, I've been wandering the land, looking up old acquaintances or their survivors, indulging the urge pathetic old folks baffled by life's swift passage sometimes feel to find out what actually happened when they were too young or too stunned to take it all in. How I got to David, who now lives in La Jolla, California, takes some explaining, as does the serpentine course of these pages. History may be linear but mem-ory, at least mine, isn't; it runs in loops.

Ben's FBI file was full of leads, old addresses and names, that en-abled me to start gathering material on the different chapters of his life, and for a while, in between conventional journalistic assign-ments, I happily passed my time contacting archivists and libraries, following those leads. I knew he had become involved with a small Communist-front organization called the League of Struggle for Negro Rights after his precipitous departure from Alabama in 1933, so I spent several afternoons at the Schomburg Center in Harlem reading the files of the *Harlem Liberator*, a short-lived weekly pub-lished by the league, and there, sure enough, I came upon an account by a former Montgomery matron of her visit with Ben to Tallapoosa County in the aftermath of a shoot-out that was portrayed in the *Montgomery Advertiser* (stridently) as well as the *Daily Worker* (triumphantly) as a Communist-inspired agrarian uprising. I knew that his first wife had a family tie to Stephen S. Wise, a formidable New York rabbi in the first half of the century who identified himself powerfully with movements of civic and social reform as well as the Zionist cause, so I read all the letters from, to, and about Ben in the Wise papers at the American Jewish Historical Society near Union Square. In an index to the hearings of the House Un-American Activities Committee over fifteen years that I came upon in the Library of Congress, I discovered that Ben's name first popped up in 1939 because of his involvement with another Communist front of the thirties, the American League Against War and Fascism (which was rechristened the American League for Peace and Democracy the day after the Nazi-Soviet pact was signed in 1939). At the film department of the Museum of Modern Art I read the unpublished memoir of a documentary film pioneer named Tom Brandon, who had traveled south to make a film on Scottsboro that never got finished and who then gave Ben his first job as a film distributor. In the basement of the Los Angeles County Court, I found the papers on Ben's name change. At the Alabama Archives in Montgomery, I found, I'm reasonably sure, most of the clippings that were in Ben's old scrapbook. On the same trip I read through old board minutes of Temple Beth Or, which when pieced together with correspondence and records I received from the American Jewish Archives in Cincinnati told the story of his ouster.

In Montgomery I also met elderly gentlemen in the Jewish community who could recall having heard Rabbi Goldstein preach or had sat in his confirmation classes and now after seventy years could still remember their fathers railing against him as an arrogant outsider with no appreciation of the social balance in the old racial order or the vulnerability of Alabama Jews. These were not emotions recalled in tranquillity; the mention of his name was enough to stir them. We're a presence in this world, it seems, until the last living child of all the people we have loved or angered has expired. Surprising as it had been to discover that an obscure figure, dead for half a century, could have left such a clear paper trail, it was a revelation to discover how unburied or close to the surface such feelings could be.

I was starting my little research project decades late. Ben's two wives long survived him, as did most of his seven siblings, but when I might have had the chance to find them, I'd no idea where to look or even what their names might be. Now, of course, they were all gone. But finding people was no longer a problem. No one can hide from the omniscient sweep of the Internet without adopting an alias and always paying cash. It took me three phone calls and a couple of e-mail messages to locate Ben's surviving daughter, Josephine Rogers, in Knoxville, where I visited her twice. I found a stepdaughter in Newton, Massachusetts, but after reminiscing fondly on the phone about the man who had married her mother she changed her mind and, furiously denouncing him in our next conversation, broke off further communication. I found two nieces in California who provided a historical sketch of the family and Ben's childhood on a farm at the edge of Sacramento where his family had moved from Oklahoma, it turned out, when he was only six years old.

Each call and stop suggested new byways for research, new books to accumulate and read, new characters with whom Ben might have come in contact, new fantasies to spin. I realized I was in danger of drowning in my research when I found myself wondering whether Ben might have consulted Scott or Zelda Fitzgerald, just returned to Montgomery from Switzerland, about a trip to Europe he was planning in 1931. (It was hardly likely but not impossible. The antiquarian sleuth I was fast becoming had discovered a society hostess who entertained the Fitzgeralds and also became close to Ben.) By then I was finally ready to confront the fact that I wasn't looking only for Ben, or even mainly for Ben. This had really been apparent from the start, but I'd put aside the question of where all this excavation was leading. Clearly I was also looking for clues to my sometimes puzzling self; my own history, my own character. Not in any sense, let me hasten to say, was I questing after the beatitude of "self-realization" and "self-discovery" promised in ashrams and such: I was too far gone and skeptical for that. I was looking for what Michael Holroyd, expressing what I take to be a kindred ambition, called "a lost narrative and sense of continuity" in a memoir I admire, *Basil Street Blues*.

Holroyd's title was a tip of the cap to W. C. Handy. I tip my cap to him. The biographer of Shaw and Lytton Strachey, he appointed himself the biographer of his parents and family in order to write what he called "a vicarious autobiography" that would fill in some of the blanks of his early life. I may share his need but lack his discipline. I'm a reporter, not a biographer. I can only go at things episodically, telling stories but not the whole story. I doubt that I'm temperamentally capable of being a biographer of my family and I've no inclination to try. I could happily interview survivors of Ben's confirmation classes in Montgomery, the sons of his trustees there, but I wasn't in the least tempted to unravel squabbles my dad had with censorious and (taking his corner, I venture to say) small-minded trustees of his Cleveland congregation who made him an icon after he died. With the passage of half a century, Ben's "lost narrative" was a reporting assignment I could easily give myself. But I could only write about my dad as part of a narrative of my own. I would not live long enough to be able to view him as other than my dad. That's to say, I'd never learn to view him from a distance in the broader scheme of his busy life.

Still, with Holroyd as an example, I wondered whether there might not be ways for me to fall back on my trade and report out some obscure moments from earlier days that have lingered as pivotal in my tattered and fallible and possibly treacherous memory. The reporter's impulse is to inquire about things that are not known or understood. Mine here has been to explore things I half understood or never grasped at all while they were happening in my boyhood, as opposed to things that happened later on which I presume to know well or, sometimes, all too well. Mainly, after detouring around the subject for most of my years, I'm now talking about knots in relation to my parents that never got untied—"hot spots," to lift a term used by radiologists who do cancer scans, of my emotional history.

Which is not to say, I hope, that it's the story of a malignancy. I think of this as a memory loop, rather than a memoir; a particular circuit of memories that I feel driven to retrace and connect, where possible, to something like an objective record or the memories of someone else, in hopes of glimpsing what was once real. I say they

form a loop simply because that's the capricious way they unravel in my mind.

Strange as it may seem, we clung to the notion that we were a happy and loving family and would not have said with Tolstoy that we were unhappy in our own way. My parents were used to performing in public. In private they also had their showstopping moments, but they had to be coaxed to perform for their sons. It was heaven when we could get my dad to launch himself into one of his renditions of "Mr. Monte Cristo," an old music hall ballad about the stranded fugitive and his vain boast, "The world is mine," on which the song heaps scorn:

> Just a barren island, he thought was divine.
> Just a lot of water, just a lot of sand,
> Mr. Monte Cristo, how on earth could that be grand?

There was never any danger that my dad wouldn't ham it up and bring down the house when he got to the last stanza:

> You had no wild, wild ladies
> Raising Hades.
> You had no liquor there.
> You had no banjo playing, serenading,
> Just some sunshine and air.
> You had no women, wine or even song
> But still you poor old chump, you went along,
> Though you were sighin', cryin',
> You know that you were lyin',
> When you said, "The World is Mine."

My mom's star turn came at the Passover seder, when Judaism finds its most noble expression not in a house of worship under the tutelage of some rabbi but in an intimate service conducted at home, by and for the family. Since our family included a rabbi who was anything but dutiful about the proceedings, we got it all, the warmth along with the theatrical panache of a pro. The seder, of course, renders the story of the flight from Egypt in the form of a ritual leading to a feast. In our household of long ago, it was always as beautifully laid out as it was performed. We used a liberal Haggadah that censored, on principle, the maledictions and plagues, including the slaying of the Egyptian firstborn, so I was shocked when as an adult in late middle age I first heard the traditional prayer that begins, "Pour out thy wrath upon the nations . . ." My mom's moment followed the meal with the recital of a roundelay of a dozen verses that goes by the numbers, a kind of Partridge in a Passover Tree. "Who knows the meaning of number one?" the leader asks, evoking the prescribed response: "One stands for the Lord our God alone." Each verse then adds another line to the one that came before as the leader asks the meaning of two, three, four, and so on up through twelve (thirteen in other Haggadahs). My dad would start by chanting a few verses in Hebrew, then, taking turns, we'd read in English. That's when it became a game, a competitive exercise in breath control. The challenge was to read your verse in a single breath. As the verses got longer, the participants read as fast as they could but still mostly ran out of air and voice, gulping for a fresh mouthful before the finish line, as vanquished as a porgy in the bottom of a skiff. Not my mom, who waited for the last and therefore longest verse.

"Who knows the meaning of number twelve?" was her cue, a signal for everyone to look her way. Her training for the stage now paid off. She never raced, beginning at an even conversational pace, with plenty of expression, "Twelve tribes from Egypt did God redeem; / Their redemption is this festival's theme. / Eleven the stars of Joseph's dream . . ." and so on without strain as she made her way down the count to a reprise of the first answer about the Lord our

God alone. When she was done, it always seemed she could have easily gone on for a few more lines without any more oxygen than she still had stored in her lungs. Every Passover, she made it look easy.

I remember, too, my parents doing the samba at the center of a dance floor at a ridiculously extravagant bar mitzvah reception at the Waldorf. All the other dancers stepped back to gape. They couldn't get over the idea that a rabbi and his wife could throw themselves into the samba with such supple, unaffected zest. I was sent to Arthur Murray's to gain that indispensable sense of release and the confidence that came with it. Someone, Arthur Murray or me, failed dismally. I admired my parents unreservedly in those days, a feeling that was easily translated into a sense that I failed to measure up, never more so than on the dance floor. Now, long after that family fragmented into separate bundles of mixed memories, tender and repressed, I'm moved to recapture a little of those times—and my long-buried feelings about them—if only to avoid having to dwell on these stories of my youth in my dotage as my avid and obsessive mother, in flight from her perpetual sense of being at fault, daily and sometimes hourly harped on hers in her last years.

It was not obvious how you went about reporting on your long-gone childhood, even if all you wanted was a slice. What was obvious, as soon as I indulged myself in the attempt, was that my surest, clearest memories had long since been heavily edited and now had to be revised. Of these, the one that probably had the strongest grip on me, the key to all my memories of Ben, concerned a clash that occurred, the way I always remembered it, a week or two after he was fired by my dad, at the bar mitzvah of a classmate of mine named Bobby Schoenfeld. Having conferred manhood on Bobby, the rabbi, a leonine figure named Louis Newman who was privately written off in our family as a windbag, yanked his homily around to the menace of McCarthyism and then, looking straight at my father, who had accompanied me to the service, mournfully bemoaned the spread of the disease to what he called "our own beloved B'nai Brith Hillel Foundations." Normally Dad was exceptionally slow to anger. But now he flushed and leaned forward suddenly, gripping the pew in front of us with both hands. Up to then, I'd never heard anyone speak of knuckles turning white, but when I eventually did I thought of that moment. Never had I seen him so furious. Later he said he had been about to rise and reply, availing himself of what he called his "Talmudic right," when he checked himself with the realization that he'd be spoiling Bobby Schoenfeld's big day. When the service ended, he rushed up to Newman and wagged a finger in his face, telling him that his charges were as reckless as McCarthy's. Loyally and proudly, I sided with my dad.

That film still runs in my mind, but now I realize it's an adaptation. Ever the reporter, I traced Bobby Schoenfeld on the Internet and sent him an e-mail. Soon we were on the phone together, only fifty-one years after we'd last talked. He was now living in Lockport, New York, retired as an engineer from Eastman Kodak. I asked him what he remembered of his bar mitzvah. He remembered that he had to memorize his whole portion because he couldn't read Hebrew and that in the last weeks of preparation the portion suddenly doubled in length because another kid who was supposed to share it dropped out. I asked him if he remembered the date. He said it had to be October. No, I said, knowing that Ben had been ousted in December, it had to be December or January. Then I asked Temple Rodeph Sholom, situated a few blocks from where I now live, whether I could check its old bulletins. The old bulletins were being rebound, but when they came back from the bindery the date turned out to have been October 28, 1950. Bobby Schoenfeld had been right, except in his insistence that it was the year of Bobby Thomson's home run; the memory boy knew that was 1951. But on the point that now mattered to me, I was clearly wrong.

The clash between my father and his rabbi was news of slight interest to the retired engineer in Lockport but news nonetheless. It had been sufficiently elliptical to pass unnoticed by Bobby, his family, and the rest of the congregation, but I hadn't imagined it. Now that I knew that it had preceded the cashiering of Ben, I had to reconsider what had actually happened that autumn between my friend Ben and my dad and, therefore, between Ben and me. The issue couldn't have come up all at once. It must have simmered. I may already have taken sides. I may even have felt estranged from Ben, a feeling I can't recall ever having had. And that may have been how I had gotten so deeply that same autumn into ideological disputation with David Zipser, whom I now sought out in La Jolla. David, whose parents were unapologetic and active Communist Party members, had memories that forced further amendment in mine. Yes, I was finding, it was possible to do a reporting job on your childhood, not to the point of total recall of course, but at least to a point where you could begin to see the cunning and willfulness of the selections on your own personal memory console.

Finally, after these and similar encounters, I found enough courage to begin reading the letters I'd recovered from the old camp trunk in the basement. My feeling of not being from this place, I was then reminded, didn't start with our departure from Omaha. And it wasn't really about place.

2

A GREAT DISAPPOINTMENT

Considering what was going on across Europe in the same seasons, it would be nothing short of sacrilege to assert that I became a refugee in and finally from Nebraska during the summers of the Second World War. It would be equally absurd to draw a comparison between my situation and that of children who saw their fathers in those same years go off to combat, maybe never to return. My dad was a conscientious objector, a founding member as a young rabbi of a group called the Jewish Peace Fellowship. With perfect principle and futility, the Jewish Peace Fellowship aligned itself after Dunkirk and the fall of France with the Fellowship for Reconciliation, a pacifist movement with its own history of principled and, obviously, futile opposition to war (having started as an ecumenical effort among British churches after the slaughter of the original Great War had begun). At the ages of five, six, and seven I didn't know enough to ask what kind of peace the fellowships were hoping for, now that Nazi dominion stretched across Europe. Not only was I the only Jew in my Omaha classes, I was the only student who refrained from investing his nickels and dimes in "war stamps" to support the war effort. Instead, I bought "peace stamps" issued by the American Friends Service Committee to support conscientious objectors in work camps.

One of my two Alabama uncles was drafted; a cousin of the other earned his pilot's wings and then died in a military crash in

Florida before ever seeing combat. I'd never heard of my uncle's cousin until he perished, but I clung to his memory as somber proof that my family had made its sacrifice too. Troop trains passed through Omaha and on D-Day my mom, sending me on an errand to the grocer down the hill behind our house, gave me words to use in expressing my hope that his soldier son wouldn't be harmed in the invasion. I doubt that we had yet heard of Omaha Beach but I knew the meaning of the small gold-star banners I occasionally glimpsed in the parlor windows of houses in our neighborhood. And in the basement of our second Omaha home on South 35th Avenue, I patiently glued together small pieces of balsa wood, purchased in kits, to make model Spitfires and P-47s, oblivious as far as I can recall of any contradiction between the symbolism of such artifacts and my "peace stamps."

For a well-fed, well-clothed, well-housed youngster near the placid center of the continent in a pre-television age, war was a concept that was hard to grasp, a darkness that was always remote but never quite absent. It had little or nothing to do with the surprising personal outcome of those years for me. Despite the cushioning I could take for granted, I ended the war years with the soul of a refugee after all. Often unsure of where I would be living or with whom, of when I would next see my dad or whether I would ever see my parents together again, I became guarded, pensive, and, for a child my age, unusually but not happily self-sufficient.

Until I gave myself permission to start reading letters that I salvaged from the camp trunk, I had little in the way of a narrative for those years, only an itinerary. My memories were limited to a paltry number of frozen tableaux, scenes in which nothing much happened until a surge of feeling obscured them like an eclipse; static scenes on which I couldn't or wouldn't dwell. I am in a speedboat in Alabama. I am facing some bigger kids in an alley next to a movie theater on Fort Washington Avenue in New York. I'm on a farm in

Nebraska. I find my mother and little brother sitting on the edge of a bed weeping because a falling window has just smashed his finger. I'm on a slow-moving train leaving Omaha, peering down at the floodlit banks of the swollen Missouri where men are filling sandbags. I come back from the second grade in Brooklyn and try out some words on my grandma that I'd never heard in Omaha. The words are "fuckin' bastard."

My grandma laughed in my face, realizing after her initial few seconds of amazement and shock that I hadn't the slightest idea of what the words meant. So that one became a funny anecdote, but there was never anything funny in the memory tableaux that always packed the strongest emotional charge for me, the ones connected to the small, struggling Nebraska farmstead to which I was abruptly exiled for a few months the summer after my sixth birthday. I'm huddled at the top of the stairs in the small farmhouse as my dad speaks to Mrs. Jensen, the farmer's wife, in the parlor downstairs. "Treat him the way you treat your own children," I hear him saying. This is hardwired to a memory of me squirming on the backseat of a stuffy, hot sedan parked slantwise on the wide main street of a nameless town. I'm squirming because I need to go to the toilet and don't know when Mrs. Jensen will get back from her errands. By the time she returns, it's too late; I've wet myself and also left a dark telltale stain on the musty beige seat. The tableau always fades before I discover whether I've been scolded or spanked, but it's tinged

with a feeling of resentment, a sense of having been stranded and
set up for humiliation. It's the summer of 1943 and my family is somewhere else, far away. Probably an attempt has been made to furnish
me with an explanation for this state of affairs, but if so, it didn't
take. I still don't know why I'm here and not there.

In another tableau from that same time, I'm taking religious instruction on a Saturday morning in the basement of a small Seventh-
Day Adventist church where I am praised for my aptitude. I'm not
sure why I'm having to learn a second religion, whether that could
possibly have been part of what my father intended. When I finally
got to ask him, the answer was that I had been on the receiving end
of a rich experience. It wasn't an answer I could parse until very recently, when I finally made a connection between my lessons in the
Adventist basement and a lecture I heard in a college course years
later. The lecture was on the Millerites, followers of an itinerant
evangelist in upstate New York named William Miller who had the
gumption, on the basis of his scriptural readings, to proclaim the
precise date of the Second Coming, a day that would literally mark
the end of time, when all believers would ascend to heaven and non-
believers would be cast down to the eternal tortures they deserved.
For several years William Miller had preached that the Advent would
come in the first three months of 1844. When it didn't, the faith of
his followers was shaken. But this honest zealot went back to the
Scriptures and recalculated, emerging from his studies to declare the
date: October 22, 1844. Across New York and adjacent states the remaining faithful gathered by the thousands to await the Judgment
(many in white gowns, so my college lecturer said). When the sun
rose on an altogether ordinary October 23rd with no discernible
change in the earthbound lives of the would-be saints, except for
those who'd sold off their earthly possessions to support the movement, mobs gathered to sack Millerite meeting places. But a remnant
of "saints" was stalwart; it held together and regrouped, eventually

forming the Seventh-Day Adventist Church, to which Lawrence Jensen's father, a Danish immigrant of Lutheran faith who had come to Nebraska to escape conscription, eventually converted. The failure of William Miller's forecast is known by Adventists as the Great Disappointment. Those Saturday morning classes in the basement of the little whitewashed church on the crest of a hill near the Jensen farm were an introduction to the millennial spirit in our land, but all that, of course, passed over my head.

Yet in one small earthbound life, the summer of 1943 came to stand for a great disappointment all its own, as the time I inexplicably became a burden to my parents. Afterward, on occasions when I was moved to touch on my experience on the farm in talking to them, I'd usually try to keep a light tone so I'd sound as if I were kidding, just kidding, when I dropped the megaton word "abandoned" (as in, "When you *abandoned* me on the farm . . ."). But, of course, I wasn't kidding. Decades later, out of lingering grievance or spite, I still managed to work in that word.

By then I couldn't remember how I got to the farm, how long I stayed, how many Jensen children there were, or the name of the nearby town; and except for Barbara, our live-in babysitter who had taken over the part of the third floor where my Union Pacific electric train set had previously been laid out in our first Omaha home on Harney Street, I couldn't remember the names of any of the Jensens. Now that I've sifted through the letters and deployed the Internet to put myself in touch with some surviving Jensens, I know that the town was Tekamah, a little more than an hour north of Omaha; that Barbara was in Manhattan that summer with my mom and little brother; that her parents had allowed her to stay with us because Jews were presumed to be "Sabbath keepers" and abstainers from pork like the Adventists (in fact, bacon was not unknown in our household); that there were five Jensen children left on the farm, the youngest of whom were the only sons, Lawrence Jr. and Layton;

that Larry lives in Missouri and that Layton, now called Dick, is a real estate developer near Phoenix; that I was called "Joey" by the girls, who, especially Betty, had to handle most of the chores because Mr. Jensen had been laid low by crippling arthritis; that Mrs. Jenson indeed got angry and sometimes scolded severely; and that I was on the farm from early June until after the oats had been bound, shocked (that is, stacked), and threshed on a soon-to-be-obsolete threshing machine in the latter part of August, seeing my dad only twice: first after a month and a half, when I was taken to Omaha and deposited in his study at the temple for an afternoon so Mrs. Jensen could visit her husband, who'd been hospitalized nearby; and then a week later when he made his one visit to me at the farm.

Even before I returned to Tekamah after sixty years to walk the land where the old farm buildings no longer stand, this reacquired data "cued," or rather blasted loose, a jumble of frozen memories, and I could once again recall going down with Layton into the dank cool of the detached storm cellar to get relief from the hot summer sun; the kerosene lamps being turned down not long after darkness fell outside the as-yet-unelectrified house; sitting on a stool to milk one of the eight cows by hand; the unaccustomed, slightly off-putting tang of fresh, unpasteurized milk; the first taste I ever had of warm bread just out of an oven; the rusting windmill and the pump where water had to be fetched; the outhouse, a two-holer; the pigpen—eating the animals was one thing, raising them another—and the occasional chicken running around without its head after it had met the ax. Then, when I lifted my eyes from the farmyard, there were the slopes of corn and oats beyond the creek where a crowd of neighbors descended on a scalding August day to help with the threshing and revel in the reward of a picnic feast. And rediscovering all this, I discovered that I wasn't lonely, sad, and miserable every minute and hour in that summer long ago, that there were times when I didn't feel displaced, when I was actually happy, excited by a sense that "Joey" had begun to win a bit of acceptance as someone who belonged on the farm. With that realization, I'm finally able to think of the summer of 1943 without resentment, possibly for the first time since I left Tekamah, and to feel myself honorary kin with the keepers of the Jensen family history and faith. These are Betty Jensen Petersen, now of Grand Island, Nebraska—my "foster sister," by her own description, and the last of the family I knew still living in the state—and her cousin Gerald Jensen, still of Tekamah (more precisely, of the Silver Creek community of Adventists that centered on the little church on the hill, nine miles north of town on the highway and about three miles west).

A couple of weeks after I landed at the farm in June 1943 I was summoned to the windup party-line phone to take my first call from my dad. As he then recounted it in a letter he sat down to write to my mom moments later, I told him I'd been "helping Mr. Jensen get the mud off the old Ford." The day before I'd been helping with wallpapering. The point of the wallpapering, I now know, was not decorative. It was to keep the wind and rain out of the old rented farmhouse whose shingled outer shell was pocked with gaps that the howling storms of the Nebraska winter would find. Some leaks may have become noticeable as well in the summer of 1943; it was evidently a wet one. My dad got his Studebaker stuck in the mud of an unpaved county road on his one visit and had to hike the rest of the way to the farm. In his eyewitness dispatch to New York, he describes me as "one of the family" (meaning the Jensen family), in overalls and barefoot like the other boys. I am "skinny and brown and," he tells my mother, "possibly not as clean as you would have him (dirt under the fingernails and not so scrubbed behind the ears)."

"Jo's speech is definitely rural Nebraska," he goes on, using an orthography insisted on by my mother, who wanted me to style myself after the sculptor Jo Davidson, an affectation that even then I refused to indulge. He then offers a "sample conversation" with stage directions:

Jo (to Betty): Why don't you take the cultivator off the tractor?

Betty: I'll wait 'til Daddy comes home.

Jo's Dad: What's a cultivator?

Jo: Why, it's for cultivatin'.

Jo's Dad: What's cultivatin'?

Jo (with scorn): Loosenin' up the dirt around the corn and diggin' out the pig weeds.

Mom writes back that she was "relieved" to get that letter. "Still," she says, "I don't see him clearly. I'll be relieved when I do, actually." The soft fall of that "actually," a note of surprise in the middle of her New York summer, suggests that she has been momentarily caught unawares by a suppressed instinct. It's the tip-off to the narrative I found in the letters. There's a reason my dad is so determined that summer to sound like a cheerleader for the Tekamah 4-H Council. The first hairline fissure has started to show in the smooth surface of their marriage, then in its tenth year.

On the eve of her wedding in 1933 my mother had not only fallen in love with the man she was rushing headlong to marry (the date had to be advanced nine months because the original idea of waiting simply could not be endured), she'd fallen in love with the dream of being a wife to a rabbi who, she felt sure, would prove to be warm and high-minded, committed and brave. One of a kind, with her at his side.

Neither of my parents came from observant families, and later my father could never isolate one experience or influence that accounted for his surprising sense of vocation, of having heard a call. It just felt right to him, a way, or so I now speculate, of filling a void in values or identity that he sensed in his own family. While it was his choice, it's my mother who's consumed by a vision of how their lives will be after he's finally ordained. "I wish it were five years from now, darling. You'll show them vigorous thinking, no dodging—I can see it all so clearly, can't you, angel?" she writes to her fiancé, who has just started his seminary studies in Cincinnati, after she has listened to a Brooklyn rabbi waffle through a pointless sermon. "You'll be intellectually honest and although your congregation won't be more intelligent than most, they'll grow mentally while you're with them." He's then twenty; a half year older, she's barely twenty-one.

Her vision of their future isn't limited to the uplift of my dad's preaching. It's comprehensive, down to the last detail of the rabbinic house beautiful. In daily letters to her "Angelest" and "Darlingest," she dreams of the "heavenly place" where he'll have his first pulpit and excuses herself for overspending on embroidered guest towels and cocktail napkins. In making her choices, she explains, she tries to imagine how they'll look to "members of our congregation." So what if the two of them are now students and nearly penniless. She has a fixed idea of what she wants the members in that heavenly place to think, which is why she can't compromise on quality. On the way home from the future Lelyveld residence, the soon-to-be bride prophesies, wives will say to their husbands, "Do you know, our rabbi and his wife have good taste."

Ten years later, having achieved all this in Omaha, she found her life less fulfilling than she had imagined. What congregants had to say about her guest towels would never be an altogether trivial matter for her, but pleasing them was no longer a high priority. She felt stymied or, worse, trapped. Understandably, her restless imagination now needed to fasten on a destiny of her own, and for that, she felt, she needed higher degrees in what she meant to be her specialty, dramatic literature. From an early age she had been subjected to elocution lessons and pushed by her ambitious mother to sing and give recitations in front of adult as well as juvenile audiences. On Washington's Birthday in 1922, when she was nine, for instance, she was listed on a program for the children of immigrants at a vaudeville theater in the South Bronx called the Franklin. Toby Bookholtz, it said, would render patriotic songs. My mom's mom had a vision: her daughter front and center on the stage; herself hovering in the wings, managing a career. A year or two after the Franklin, Gussie Bookholtz had a studio photographer snap her Toby in a series of poses—imploring, fetching, playful—designed to pluck the heartstrings of the most hardbitten theatrical agent. Later, lacking the confidence, the sheer brio, to commit herself to a career in the theater, my mom gave elocution lesions herself for a buck an hour to other immigrants' children seeking intonations and accents that wouldn't broadcast their origins. After marrying and settling in Cincinnati, she performed in amateur theater and got an encouraging letter, special delivery, from Clifford Odets about a production of *Awake and Sing!* she directed the year I was born. ("Broadway is not America," the playwright wrote, "and I get from your present production of *Awake* an extremely satisfying sense of writing for America, a sense which fortifies me in my purposes as writer and citizen.") The Jewish Center on Reading Road in Cincinnati may not have been exactly at the heart of the heartland, but if it could seem that way to Odets in Greenwich Village, a girl from Washington Heights must have felt she was getting somewhere. Of course, she also knew that an academic career would seem more becoming for an aspiring *rebbetzin* than any conceivable life in the theater.

The higher degrees on which she set her sights were rumored to be available west of the Hudson and even west of the Missouri, but my dad agreed without hesitation that she should return to Columbia in successive summers to take courses. My intuition that I'd become a burden was not, in this context, childish invention. It's there clearly in the letters, a theme of the narrative. Exiling me to Tekamah as a young pioneer was my city-bred dad's way of trying to make things right for everyone, for now he was getting his first glimpse of how wrong they could go.

From my present perch, which gives me an overview of the

whole landscape of my parents' now completed lives, I feel a welling up of sympathy for each of them, for my mother's need to break out and my dad's desire to appease it. After all, as an instinctive concil-iator who shuns confrontation and an inveterate vagabond who has regularly given way to the impulse to break out, I take after both of them. Nevertheless, it was a little startling to come upon evidence in my mom's own words and hand that she had, in truth, begun to find me unbearable the summer after I turned five.

Take her description of the speedboat ride in Alabama that I'd recalled only dimly. I didn't know when it happened, or if it really had happened. And I'd blanked out what should have been the most memorable part of the experience, my time at the wheel. It turns out that en route from Omaha to New York, my mother, my infant brother, and I detoured to Alabama in the summer of 1942 to visit her two sisters, who'd both married men from the Muscle Shoals area, part of the Tennessee Valley development. On my brother's first birth-day, my mom and I went out on the Tennessee River in a friend's Chris-Craft. "Your elder son," she reported to my dad in Omaha, "steered the thing unassisted for more than a quarter of an hour back and forth under the old and new bridges, with an assurance that was maddening and an ability that was frightening."

All these years later, that "maddening" gets my attention. I know my mother was never careless in her choice of words, but at the dis-tance of almost a lifetime, I can't begin to grasp what she thought she'd seen in the little boy who was so enthralled at the wheel: some-thing autonomous and unreachable, I guess; a streak of willfulness, perhaps a hint of defiance. Once in New York that summer, I was promptly enrolled in a nursery at the Riverside Church. My mom writes that I'm "the loudest child there." My dad apparently sug-gests that maybe I'm a leader. "Yes," my mom replies, "Jo is a leader all right. Also he's worse every day as far as I'm concerned. I'm really at my wit's end because he's so constantly rebellious." My dad suggests she deposit me with his parents in Brooklyn in order to buy herself some peace and quiet in the cramped Washington Heights apartment of her family, which she'd fled nine years earlier but where we've now pitched up. When it's time for me to return from Brooklyn, she writes that she's "dreading the thought of coping with the noise again." When I'm roughed up by four older kids in an alley and deprived of seven cents I'd had to spend on candy, Dad stays on the subject, asking questions in successive letters: Was I scared? Did I cry? Did I fight back? The questions go unanswered while my mom presses him to hire a maid to look after me by the time she returns to Omaha.

Perhaps I was particularly obnoxious that summer, more voluble and demanding than other five-year-olds. But something deeper than the problem of a bratty kid seemed to be undermining my mother. Within a few months, the dissatisfaction she had fastened on me attaches, for the first time, to my dad. In December he takes a trip to Chicago. It's a gloomy journey because they'd quarreled at the train station (partly over his failure, it seems, to shield her from me). "Toby girl," his first letter began, "I don't know if you want me to write . . . I know I must be guilty in some way but you know too that it's not because of intent. As for Joseph, I know he's difficult—but I hope he's been behaving well enough thus far to give you some reassurance . . ." In his readiness to accept condemnation while professing not to understand the reasons for it, my dad sets the tone for much of the remaining twenty-one years of their marriage. The breezy plaintiveness with which he ends this letter will become almost reflexive. He will continue to write corny, heartfelt poems on Valentine's Day right to the end and enclose little cards with sentimental sweet nothings in the gifts he regularly brings home from his travels. And all of these my sometimes unreachable, sometimes self-punishing, often needy mother will carefully bundle and save. "Love you," he now signs off, "even tho you don't care very much for me—can't help it."

By that spring it begins to seem that Mom's restlessness has infected Dad; either that or the departure of contemporaries and close friends for overseas combat zones has led him to question whether the huge issues of war and peace are most usefully addressed from an Omaha pulpit. He has just turned thirty, an age at which, even in settled times, the question of whether you're on the right road becomes almost inescapable. His congregation indulges him when he preaches on the Gandhian vision, but in the end, it is only a sermon. These Omaha merchants and professionals are not prepared to change their lives in any basic way. But he stands ready, at least for a while. Looking for some deeper engagement, he has gone to an army post near Lincoln, Nebraska, where he uses his clergyman's privilege to investigate the case of a private from New York named Levy who has been disciplined for sounding off on the treatment of black soldiers. My dad is on a mission for the Workers Defense League, a group in the anti-Communist sector of the labor movement that concerns itself with the rights of draftees; the case turns out to be a little murkier than he'd been given to believe, and the solution is to cut short, rather than step up, a campaign on behalf of Private Levy for which the league had already printed leaflets and sent out press releases back East. A couple of months later he interviews a conscientious objector in Chicago and writes a letter to the governor of Nebraska at the urging of a black newspaper editor. He also serves on the local Urban League board. But this is all secondhand and occasional. So in March he goes to Philadelphia to call at the American Friends Service Committee, to inquire about "overseas opportunities" and put his name on a list of volunteers. He says he's interested in China and North Africa, also Mexico, and talks of taking courses at Columbia that would give him qualifications for work in postwar reconstruction programs. In May, at a pacifists' conference on Lake Winona in Indiana, he's again having conversations on "opportunities for foreign service." His new idea is to head a "Jewish relief unit" in Europe made up of conscientious objectors.

None of this, then or later, ever trickled down to his sons. Never once did he mention that he had briefly thought himself ready to fly the hump to wartime Chungking. Yet it's obviously something my parents had discussed. My father doesn't find it necessary to explain in these letters what would happen to my mother or us. My guess is that they had an understanding: if he picked up stakes in Omaha, she would too, heading straight for New York. Soon she's asking how come it's a problem when she talks of moving on but no problem when he does. After that, his impulse to do good works abroad never gets mentioned again by either of them.

By the summer of 1943, with me safely out of range with the Adventists in Tekamah, he must have realized he was taking over as the obstacle to her happiness and fulfillment; if it wasn't specifically him, it was the nexus of obligations and duties that my dad and their sons had come to represent in her mind. As my Tekamah summer unfolded, Mom came to sound alternately whimsical and taunting, distant and aggrieved in her letters to Dad. Back in the summer of 1942, when the time drew near for her to put Manhattan behind her and return to her comparatively staid, overscheduled Omaha life as a rabbinical spouse, she had still found it in herself to compose a paean to that life. "I've got a beautiful Arthur," she wrote then, "2 gorgeous boys, just the house we want, the clothes I like and I'm ready to begin the year ahead with people we like. How odd of me!" The next summer it's the world of seminars and dissertation advisers on Morningside Heights that becomes the subject of her paeans. "I'm in a world I adore," she writes. "It gives me a great lift—I'm happy and comfortable in it. I feel I'm doing well. People think I'm o.k. I feel attractive." She has to admit the truth. She just loves "being alone and on my own." That's why she can't make herself write what he yearns to hear, that she's lonely and misses him. Instead, she writes with evident excitement about the attention she has been getting from one of her professors, a suave and ironic Renaissance scholar named Maurice Valency who becomes "V" in her letters. After "V" has been mentioned a couple of times, Dad admits to pangs of jealousy. She tells him he's "a silly." A decade later Valency and his wife, Janet, would move into our apartment house and we'd come to know him as Val. He was making a name for himself by then beyond the academic cloister, adapting Giraudoux for Audrey Hepburn on Broadway, Dürrenmatt for the Lunts, and Offenbach for the Metropolitan Opera. His professorial chair, house in the Caribbean, and Jaguar sports car had not yet materialized in 1943. With a worldliness that might have sounded a bit too offhand in Omaha, my mom writes to my suspicious dad that "V" would be quite a conquest but "I am very much married to you."

Letters have crossed and he has taken her more seriously than she probably intended when she started to tease him with the idea of staying on in New York. It would be a saving on railway fare, she had written, and, ever the language snob, added that "Jo could have his dialect ironed out in no time at Horace Mann." Her real complaint has been that once again he hasn't succeeded in hiring a maid, which shows he doesn't take her professional quest for a doctorate as seriously as she takes his work. Come to think of it, she says, he's so settled and absorbed in what he does that her absence wouldn't matter much to him at all. He hastens to prove her wrong on both counts, urging her to stay on if that is what she feels she must do. "The only thing you have in Nebraska is me—and that may not be good enough," he writes, once again sounding abject in hopes, it seems clear, of winning a little tenderness in the form of a contradiction. What he gets is a gentle chiding and a touch of sarcasm. She lets him know that she has seriously considered staying, "spent more sleepless nights over it than you can guess," but she's coming home. She also lets him know that she isn't reconciled to that fate. "It's just a cockeyed convention," she writes, "that takes me to Omaha or to Oshkosh or wherever you happen to be while you couldn't budge from such a place to be with me, say, in N.Y."

"You'll feel better," she says in her last letter from New York that summer of '43, "when I'm back at my chores, starting Saturday." My mom was adept at finding words that sting ("chores," in this instance) but my dad must have felt relieved.

Considering how bitter I came to be about my banishment to Tekamah, I should have a vivid memory of my return to my family in Omaha, which seems to have coincided with the return of my mom and brother from New York. But I've no memory of that at all. I also have no memory of our move to South 35th Avenue late in September after our landlord suddenly put the Harney Street house, with its high lilac hedge, on the market. When we'd first moved to Harney Street two years earlier, I'd pined for Ohio the way I would later pine for Omaha when we moved to New York. I have a blurry memory of having kept a souvenir of the new Cincinnati train station in my small room hard by the stairs to the attic, but whether it was one of those little inverted bowls that magically produce snow when you turn them upside down, a model of molded bronze, or a mere pennant I can no longer say. Somewhere in that precocious sense of loss and transience were, I suspect, the makings of a foreign correspondent. A pattern had been set: by the time I was six, I was used to not being from this place, wherever this place happened to be. But I'd settled into the neighborhood and found friends like Mason, who led me through several chambers impressively dug out of a frozen snowdrift, and Tommy, who got run over by a car but luckily only cracked some ribs when he took his sled down his icy driveway and then found he couldn't stop at the big street by Elmwood Park. Now our latest move had thrust me into first grade in a new school in another part of town where I knew no one.

Here's an example of how memory, at least my memory, sets its own scene, casting aside whatever doesn't fit its story line. My story line for the time after my summer on the farm always skipped over the disruption that for a six-year-old so clearly had to be involved in the move to a new neighborhood. It went like this: The family was now happily reunited and I was home safe and sound. So in my memory, the new house on South 35th Avenue—a spacious three-story red-brick structure with a central hall opening onto a dining room on the left and a living room on the right—became our ancestral home, the unshadowed and settled scene of an idyllic childhood. For years, in my imagination, a kind of timelessness attached to it. There every Sunday evening, in a family ritual I remember as immutable, I'd be served the same dinner—runny soft-boiled eggs with little pieces of toast mixed in and pudding, usually tapioca, my favorite—while I sat on a couch on the small windowed porch off the living room and listened to the Jack Benny radio show. Sunday evening was the one evening in the week I could be sure both my parents would be home. It was, had been, and always would be so; at least that's the feeling I retained. Memory had a way of getting stuck on those serene Sunday evenings on South 35th Avenue, refusing to move forward or back.

What a dream. In fact, we lived in the brick house there for only nine months and the Sunday evenings that were the emotional pivot of my remembered idyll could hardly have happened the way I remembered as many as ten weeks in a row. What I found in the trunk revealed key dates and showed me a story line that veered sharply from the one on which I'd relied. My idyll, I discovered, had been willfully pieced together out of a time of tumult in our household. Other pictures, long suppressed, then came back to me, another layer of cued memories.

The high-spirited assertiveness Mom brought back from New York shattered within a couple of months. At first she threw herself into a fever of decoration, restoring old pieces of furniture in order to bring our new home up to her standards. I remember her down in the basement for hours at a time, next to the laundry sink, intently sanding and varnishing the scruffy foundlings and waifs she rescued

from used furniture shops and converted with her own fierce energy
into gleaming "antiques." I remember her excitement when uphol-
sterers brought back a severe cherrywood settee with scrolled arms
that she'd had re-covered in a heavy printed cotton, a sort of substi-
tute chintz, crawling with the thorny branches, leaves, and red blos-
soms of a rosebush. My dad called it "Fanny Fracture" and the name
stuck. Then, not long after everything was finally in place, less than
two months after we'd moved in, she suffered a breakdown over
which a curtain was hastily drawn. My guess is that it involved an
overdose, probably more in the way of a gesture than a serious attempt on her life, but if I was told anything at all, it would have been
the vague story given the world, meaning the Temple Israel congregation: the rabbi's wife was overtired and had checked herself into a
hospital to get a rest. A week before Thanksgiving, my dad sent a
telegram to Des Moines canceling a talk to a temple sisterhood
there that my mother had been scheduled to give. "It became imperative for Mrs. Lelyveld to withdraw from all activities for at least
the next few weeks," he wrote in a follow-up letter supposedly offering a fuller explanation but adding only more words.

A few weeks later everything is again up in the air, including the
question of where I will now live and with whom. My pregnant aunt
from Alabama is looking after my brother and me in the new house.
My mother's mother is preparing to come to Omaha to relieve my
aunt. Dad's dad is writing to ask "what is going on in Omaha at the
home of the Lelyvelds." My mother is once again discussing the
idea of moving to New York with the children, which would mean
yanking me out of my new school. Meanwhile, she's holed up in a
hotel near Lincoln Park in Chicago where my dad stops to visit her on
his way to meetings in Cleveland and Cincinnati. Before he arrives,
she writes promising to meet him at the station and suggesting they
go dancing. After he leaves she sends a drowsily good-humored letter saying she realizes "the game is up" and that it's time for her to

"get back on the job." Unless, she goes on in a vein that is not much more than half joking, he has found a thousand dollars or so to enable her to "stay on and on" in her hotel room, continuing what she calls her "vacation," which has involved, by her account, borrowing books from a lending library and eating by herself in a diner where strange men send her notes and try to strike up conversations. "I'm really glad you were here," the letter ends. "Now that you're gone— I love you, Toby."

By the end of 1943, it seems, I was once again getting my soft-boiled eggs on the windowed porch during Jack Benny's half hour on Sundays. I can run through the gallery of images of my dad in my memory and almost believe I see him, recall the sense of his presence, as a thirty-one-year-old Omaha rabbi. Of course, what I think I can see is a collage of photos and a reimagining of later, clearer images. But my mom is more elusive. I know that people said she was beautiful and that I always thought so. But when I try to picture her in our Omaha days all I can see is a portrait that was painted not long after she returned from Chicago by a watercolor artist named Elias Newman, a friend of my parents who, on a stop-off in Omaha, also gave them the inscribed Jerusalem landscape I was to find in the camp trunk a half century later. I can remember that the artist stayed for a night or two in the guest room next to the room I shared with my brother on South 35th Avenue, and coming home from school to find my mom sitting for him there in a fancier dress than she'd normally have been wearing in the middle of the day. In that memory, she's facing me as I stand on the threshold looking over the artist's shoulder to his easel, comparing the image taking form there to my mother's face. In all likelihood, the one was more animated than the other, for she was probably telling me she could not be interrupted. That contrast was repeated for years to come, whenever she was in the same room as her portrait. In the picture, her hair is drawn tight and piled around the crown of her head in a severe schoolmarmish bun. The face is exceptionally long, slightly green-ish in tint, and infinitely sad. It's a portrait of a mood rather than a likeness of her actual physiognomy. Her face was not exceptionally long, and when it was calm, as it appears to be in the portrait, it was usually serene in later life. As a child I hated the painting without being able to say why. If I'd had the words, I'd have said it scared me by evoking a sense of her unhappiness in our time on South 35th Avenue and of what could still happen to our family were she to be plunged into that mood again. Yet years later, when she asked what I wanted for my fiftieth birthday, I laid claim to the portrait. Now I treasure it because I know my mother always felt it had uncannily caught her own sense of herself at the time.

Slightly more than two months passed after my mom's return from her Chicago "vacation" before our next family crisis. Nothing

much happened in that time except that I had my tonsils out, narrowly escaping the removal of my appendix by a hasty surgeon who'd mistaken me for another boy. (As I was going under the ether, I muttered, "I want Dr. Greenberg to take my tonsils out." Suddenly the big light in the operating theater was switched off. Tonsils? Did someone mention tonsils?) But then my brother, at two and a half, came down with a form of pneumonia that was often fatal in small children before the introduction of antibiotics. The drug he needed was relatively new in commercial production, still in short supply, and in early 1944 earmarked exclusively for the military. Well-connected Omaha friends tried to pull strings in Washington to get a dose for Davy. With his life in the balance, my mom stayed at the hospital and I was farmed out to a fancy suburb to these same fancy friends. My dad appeared on my seventh birthday to take me to see *Snow White and the Seven Dwarfs*. We were joined by the head of the local Urban League chapter, with whom my dad sometimes played tennis, and his daughter, who was about my age. I'd seen black household servants. I think I'd even traveled to Alabama with a black maid on a train that became segregated as soon as it crossed the Ohio River. But I'd never before known we could have black friends. As far as I can recall, Dad said nothing to communicate the lesson of my birthday outing. Strange then—unless you consider that I'd grown up in America—that it struck me as a revelation and stayed with me the rest of my life.

The string-pulling seems to have failed. Davy never got the miracle drug but old-fashioned bedside care pulled him through. Finally, he came home, enabling me to come home too. Not long after that it was time again to leave Omaha for the summer. As the train chugged slowly over the railway bridge from which I viewed the men filling sandbags on the embankment of the rising Missouri River, I had no idea that I would not be returning to the brick house, that nearly thirty-two years would pass before I next set foot in Nebraska.

Yet even then, as the train sped up and headed eastward through Iowa cornfields, Omaha was becoming a figment of my imagination.

It's 1976 and I'm a reporter on assignment in Iowa at the start of a presidential campaign. The assignment gives me leeway to report anywhere I want in the state, so I choose Council Bluffs, the town across the river from Omaha. Setting off from Des Moines, I drive across Iowa and then across the Missouri into my imagined hometown. I remember my first house was near a park and I remember the walk to school. I remember the second house was near a hotel called the Blackstone and that I had to cross a broad thoroughfare a few short blocks from our home to get to my second school. Omaha is a sizable town and it has obviously changed in thirty-two years: the stockyards, the sight and fragrance of which could hardly be missed on a drive downtown, seem to have vanished. Yet without asking directions, the memory boy manages to find both houses and schools before getting out of the car to check in at the Blackstone, where as a six-year-old I'd sometimes hung out in the lobby while my father was performing weddings in the ballroom or, if it hadn't yet opened for business, in a cocktail lounge called the Cottonwood Room where the bar encircled the eponymous tree.

I toast my return there alone. I've had no reason to think even glancingly of the Cottonwood Room in all those years, but as I sit there nursing my drink the hairs on the back of my neck seem to tingle and I'm seized by a disproportionate emotion over my recognition of what seems to be an absolute lack of change in the room, as if it had been there waiting for me, a wandering Odysseus landing unheroically on his little stage set of an Ithaca. I know it's a joke, really, my pious sense of homecoming in a bar, but still I'm moved to my core.

But what, I now wonder, could it have been that moved me? Maybe it was the sense of transience in my own life, brought into relief by a recognition that I was then seven or so years older than my parents had been when they put Omaha behind us. Maybe it was that I had found a touchstone offering intimations of the story I'm now trying to piece together at a time when I felt distant, if not estranged, from my parents, who by then were bitterly estranged themselves. Whatever it was, this sad and comical weekend plunge into *les temps perdus* continued the next morning, a Sunday, with a visit to Temple Israel, the one place I ever had a sense of myself as carrying a special status and burden as "the rabbi's son." A domed Byzantine structure, it had been transformed in my absence, appropriately enough, into a Greek Orthodox church. Atop the dome there was now a Greek cross.

The easiest way to see the building from inside seemed to be to attend services. I thought little of it when an usher asked me to fill in a visitor's card. A half hour or so later I was stunned when the visitors' names were read out and we were asked to stand and come to the front of the sanctuary for a blessing. On the inside of the dome, there was now a mosaic of the Virgin in a blue robe against a field of gold. The incense was also new. There were five visitors. Four, in name and appearance, were clearly of Greek origins, while one had no apparent touch of Hellas. I smiled in embarrassment, hoping I'd be taken for a convert, perhaps someone married to a Greek. Fortunately no one asked me to state my connection, so I didn't have to choose between talking about pilgrimages to Delphi, Eleusis, and Samothrace—sites that were Greek but decidedly not Orthodox—or declaring that I'd been the rabbi's son here before the building was put under new auspices.

A couple of days later, before checking out of the Blackstone, I rang the bell at 535 South 35th Avenue, which now stood in a transitional neighborhood behind the Mutual of Omaha corporate headquarters, a looming fortress that dwarfed anonymous two-story blocks of rental apartments and one-family homes that had obviously seen better days. With a large steel fire escape affixed to its side, our old brick house had an institutional look. Two young social workers admitted me, explaining that it had become a home for youngsters described as mentally handicapped. Given the run of the place, I was followed everywhere I went by a dozen or so gurgling children clutching at my sleeves and trousers. Two discoveries jolted me with the same small shock of recognition, the same frisson, I'd gotten from the cottonwood tree in the bar. One was the deep closet in what had been my parents' bedroom. It had a single door on the right but ran the length of the wall. I remembered that I'd always thought of it as a kind of tunnel and that my collection of *National Geographic*s had been piled near its far end. The other was the laundry sink at the foot of the basement stairs, which instantly summoned thoughts of model planes and furniture restoration. A closet and a laundry sink: a genuine, solidly utilitarian, Middle American space and artifact, entirely devoid of the sensuous appeal memory might locate in a fragrant baker's confection in the shape of a small seashell. Yet each in the moment I came upon it seemed to me a discovery; a revelation, really. That evening I called my brother David, then a professor of South Asian history in Minnesota, to tell him that our old house was now a home for problem children. "So what else is new?" he shot back.

Since then I've been back to Omaha just once. It took another twenty-seven years. The old South 35th Avenue house still belonged to the Eastern Nebraska Council for the Retarded, only now it was a residence for five mentally handicapped women. Some of them, a young counselor suggested, might have been children there when I paid my first revisit. The Blackstone still stood, but as an office building now conspicuously the worse for wear. What had been the Cottonwood Room was for rent as a store. None of these landmarks exerted any great tug on my sentiments the second time around. I skipped the Greek Orthodox church, which by now had belonged to the Greeks longer than it had belonged to the Jews. Instead, I made for the farm near Tekamah.

The county road was still unpaved as it had been six decades earlier when my father got his Studebaker stuck in the mud. But this August it has scarcely rained, and even though irrigation had become a factor in Nebraska cultivation, crop estimates were slipping. I felt vindicated to find myself heading through rolling landscape, not flat prairie, having never quite believed my own recollection of oats and corn on rising slopes. But it wasn't till I came upon the little Adventist church at the top of a rise that I saw a building I could imagine I'd seen before. Gerald Jensen, the leader of the congregation, which had dwindled to about a dozen members from a high of about a hundred, lived just beyond the church in a small whitewashed house next to a barn that he hadn't bothered to rebuild after a big wind took it down a few years ago.

Now closing in on eighty but still lending a hand on his son's nearby farm, Gerald (who pronounces his name with a hard g) had the lean and limber look of a much younger man. It took just a few minutes, heading back eastward on the county road, to come to the piece of land he knew I wanted to see. There, navigating by two big cottonwood trees that had been killed in a grass fire within the past year, Gerald pointed out to me where the barn and the farmhouse had stood in the time his uncle Lawrence Jensen rented the farm, when he took a brooding six-year-old from Omaha into his family.

Standing in what had been the yard, I looked up to a slope whose contours were just as I'd imagined. A tidy expanse of ground-hugging soybean plants stretched along its crown. Down below it was chest-high grass running wild. No one could make a living anymore, Gerald said, on a 240-acre farm. The owner, having long since knocked down and burned what remained of the buildings in order to qualify for the lower tax rates on unimproved property, had put most of the acreage in a federal conservation program that paid fairly well.

I plunged into the high grass looking for traces of a foundation or a cavity suggestive of the old storm cellar but met only more high grass and thistles. There was the skeleton of an old corn crib toward the eastern edge of the property and some rusted barbed-wire fencing down by the creek, but beyond that, it would take an archaeological dig, I figured, to turn up evidence that anyone had ever threshed oats and raised livestock or a family near this spot.

It was late in the month, just the time, Gerald said, when the threshing machine and neighbors would have been summoned to bring in the crop. So here I stood—sixty years probably to the week, possibly even sixty years to the day—in communion with a homestead that had long ago finished its life span except in the imaginations of Gerald, scattered other Jensens, and me. The way I could now see this abandoned farm was the way Gerald, a man who had lived his whole life along the county road, could see the entire surrounding countryside: as a layered series of narratives of his own family and others. What I was struggling to regain, in other words, he'd never lost. And it fit right in with his Adventist theology, which has consistently taught, since the time of William Miller, that these were "the last days."

Gerald unlocked the little church, observing that it had never needed a lock till five years ago when thieves backed a truck to its door and cleared out every stick of furniture except for an old blackboard fixed to its own easel in the basement where once I'd taken religious instruction. I eyed the old blackboard, not quite convincing myself that we'd met before. Then I helped myself to an Adventist pamphlet that ticked off signs aplenty in our contemporary world of its imminent end: *Terrorism . . . surgical air strikes bringing on more terrorist raids . . . child abuse and molestation . . . the cult of self-indulgence . . . arrogant materialism . . . hoarded wealth for a few, plant closings for many . . . a veritable orgy of junk bond dealing and leveraged buyouts . . . new agers selling magical crystals and channeling departed spirits . . . earthquakes and famines.* There was a radical critique and subtext running through the pamphlet, but, of course, it offered no hope in this world. Each of these phenomena was attached to an apt citation from the Apostles, warning of "false prophets," of "wars and rumors of wars." Each foreshadowed a Second Coming slouching towards Tekamah and the wider world. *The conclusion is obvious*, the pamphlet said. *The generation portrayed by these signposts of prophecy will see Jesus return . . . It won't be long till He'll sweep away sin and suffering.*

When I got to Grand Island, Betty Petersen, the Jensen who seemed to remember "Joey" best, welcomed me with a big hug. It was the first and possibly last time in my life I would ever have a reunion with someone after sixty years. On what was for them a Sabbath morning, she and her husband, Martin, invited me back for a breakfast of waffles. By then I had caught up with the news of her immediate family. Across the decades, there had been much unhappiness, loneliness, and illness. Of course, there had also been long sunny interludes and memorable moments, but as Betty, nearing the end of her eighth decade, surveyed these earthly lives, the sum of her family's experience, it was the inevitable losses that formed the milestones. Four of her five siblings and three of her four children had been in marriages that went bad. Her much loved eldest sister, Barbara, once my babysitter, had succumbed to chronic lung disease ten years before in Tucson after a career as a teacher in the Omaha schools. Barbara's two children, whom she had followed to Arizona, had vanished as far as the rest of the family now knew. Inez, another sister, died of cancer two years later after a courageous fight. One of Betty's two sons, Keith, now had no other home besides the tractor trailer he drove across the country as he struggled to recoup savings lost in an investment that was more risky than he'd ever imagined. The other, Ronn, had died suddenly and inexplicably at the age of fifty-one. Twice a year, despite Betty's painful hip and Martin's feelings of weakness after treatment for prostate cancer, they traveled

back to Tekamah, where Ronn had never lived, to tend his grave in the peaceful little cemetery next to the Adventist church. Of all the sad things they had faced, Ronn's loss was the hardest. Yet their faith kept them buoyant and cheerful: their faith that the world will soon end. "This old world isn't going to last much longer," Betty recalled having said to her son two weeks before she lost him. As she recounted it, he replied: "I'm ready. I hope He comes tomorrow."

"That's some comfort to me," Betty said.

When Martin asked a direct question, I admitted I wasn't religious. But I couldn't bring myself to confess that I loved the world on my best days, that it contained all I really cared about in the entire cosmos, and so I'd never understood what was so soothing about the promise of its end. Eternal bliss is the answer, I realize, but it's an answer I failed to grasp when I had an opportunity, in the basement of the Adventist church near Tekamah.

Betty, who had self-published a thick treatise on Jensen genealogy with detailed essays on the recent generations, opened a family album and plucked out a snapshot from the summer of '43 of her two grinning brothers, Lawrence and Layton, flanking a sad little fellow in an embarrassingly cute sailor suit that looks as if it had been on the ironing board moments before. I couldn't have survived a Nebraska August in those clothes, so probably that was how I was got up when the time came for me to be sent home to Omaha. Was I sad because I was always sad? Or was I sad because I was being turned into a city kid again? Memory offers no clue. Perhaps I was just apprehensive about what would happen next.

3

NOT FROM THIS PLACE

Dear Father How are you Where are we Going to Live in new York or omaha

The note, painstakingly printed in a crooked, childish hand and probably dictated by my high-strung maternal grandma, was mailed from Washington Heights in New York at the end of the summer of 1944. The postmark says "Sep 1," making it the week after I arrived from Maine, where my mom had deposited me at the summer's start. I'd then found myself at a boys' camp while she stayed on, a couple of miles away, to run the drama program at the nearby girls' camp. I'd seen her for maybe fifteen or twenty minutes a week; the last time came moments before the start of a dramatic pageant that was to be the culmination of her summer's labors. (A hundred and fifty children would be taking part, she had written in a note to her sisters, calling it "the biggest thing I've ever done.") I picture her now in a tailored tweed jacket over a white blouse and forest green camp shorts. Her mood is elevated. In this recollection, pressed like a flower in the recesses of my brain, her eyes sparkle and she greets me with an unusually wide smile as if the two of us have to perform for the audience in which I'm seated near the front.

Then she vanished, seemingly, from my life. A couple of days later, a woman who worked with her came to deliver a message to me at the camp infirmary where I went regularly that summer for oatmeal baths to heal a nasty eczema rash on the inside of my thighs. (In their letters to one another, my parents attributed the eczema to nervous tension; they didn't attribute the nervous tension to anything.) The messenger said my mother hadn't been feeling well and had to go away. She didn't say where, only that someone would meet me when the camp train got to New York.

When I then wrote out the note to my dad, signing it "Joe Boy" with the stubborn *e*, I was seven years old, due to enter the second grade in little more than a week. The only question was where. Where meaning not which school but which city. At that particular point, our family was scattered to the winds. I was in New York, my brother in Alabama. My dad was in Omaha, my mom in Kansas City, where, her letters reveal, she'd taken a temporary job with an airline instructing in some subject, probably elocution. Mysteriously, she appears to have been registered at her hotel there under an alias, "E. Schell." Her aim was to make quick money, enough to secure an apartment in New York near Columbia, where she planned to start work on her dissertation. To the consternation of my four grandparents, there were still no plans for me. Four destinations had been under discussion by my parents in the previous few weeks; not just New York and Omaha but also Alabama and Denver, where my uncle had cousins, one of whom I'd come to think of as an honorary aunt ever since she'd stayed with us in Omaha. What my grandparents already knew but waited for my parents to tell me was that even if I ended up in New York, I wouldn't be living with my mom. My note had a sad little fallacy—that "we" would have to be together somewhere soon.

The absence of parents meant the absence of explanations for what was happening and not happening in my life. But then how would you explain to a seven-year-old that his mother has taken an existential decision, as she variously explained it in letters to my dad, to rediscover her "simple and honest drives"; to "do it alone"; "to be myself"; living with "no plans, no hopes, no desires for the future"? My mom's letters that summer proclaimed a state of calm certitude; between the lines was a fragile determination that could be defined as courage. She knew what she was doing. It would be best for all of us, especially for my father, who would gain the "serenity and relief" he could never have with her. She could not take his money. She had funds of her own set aside with which to launch herself into a new life. A grand total of fifty-five dollars, it turned out. For the first time the word "divorce" appeared in one of her letters. She didn't ask for one but hinted that if my dad felt he needed such a resolution, he'd meet no resistance. My dad tells her that she is "not reacting normally," that they should seek psychiatric counseling together. Seldom a brooder himself, he warns her against "unhealthy self-preoccupation." All he gets in response are expressions of regret for the problems she has heaped on him. For a brief spell, her certitude seems to outlast his doubts. "I am not going to impose myself on you any longer," he writes, "but I want you to know I shall never close the door completely nor change my feeling for you." Never, as a commitment, is unending. He would manage to keep that pledge for another twenty years, not a short time.

So that's how the discussions of an abode and schools for me began. My dad was back in Omaha after spending the summer barnstorming across the country on behalf of the Zionist Organization of America. He proposed that I stay with his parents in Brooklyn and go to school there. My mom, who clearly didn't want to have to face all over again, every day, her decision to shun me, said New York was out of the question. So she convinced herself that she was the cause of whatever problems I might have, writing to her sisters that "he is never anything but calm and sweet and cooperative except when he sees me." To my father, she wrote, "Jo *must* not have any of the tensions that made me me. Please." Taking herself out of my life, at least for a time, would achieve this end, or so she seems to be arguing. Her position was that my dad should stay in Omaha and I should stay there too with my brother, who was then just three.

My dad seemed to be bending to her view when suddenly her calm crumbled, her resolve snapped, as a result of a bombshell letter she got from her uncomprehending parents, who scolded her about ruining not only her own life but the lives of a devoted husband and two sons. Her craving for solitude and what she thought of as independence—flickering sometimes but inextinguishable over many years—they saw as a dark compulsion, something gone haywire. "O.K., you're all of you right," my mom then wrote to my dad, momentarily lumping him into the parental conspiracy to corral her. "If you will still have me, I'll come back to Omaha." He spoke to her on the phone and heard the confusion, verging on desperation, in her voice. But he would not accept her surrender so easily this time. She'd made her case for independence better than she knew and, in fact, had been home only eight of the previous fifteen months. "I won't again be guilty of pushing you into a way of life not of your own choice," he wrote. It was on receipt of that letter that she'd fled Maine—and me—turning up at the tip of Cape Cod, in Provincetown.

"Joe Boy," in New York, knew next to nothing of all this. He only knew that he was stranded again. Within a week after I wrote my pathetic little note to my dad, I was living on Ocean Parkway in Brooklyn with my Lelyveld grandparents, enrolled at P.S. 238 near Kings Highway. That outcome was a compromise, designed by my dad and accepted by my mom at a rendezvous at the Hotel Muehlebach in Kansas City, their first face-to-face discussion in two months. Since they were finally meeting, the compromise did not have to be written down, but its outlines soon became apparent. My mom would get her independent life near Columbia but not the distance from husband and children she had craved. She would also start seeing a psychiatrist. My brother would stay mostly with her parents in

Washington Heights while I was in Brooklyn. But on weekends we could be traded back and forth. My dad's dad had tried to head off this obviously makeshift solution. He and my grandma didn't feel up to the round-the-clock burden of children in their small one-bedroom apartment. It would be "too much for Mother," he had written, urging that we be kept in Omaha: my grandma, a loving but somewhat phlegmatic woman then in her fifties, would become ill, he said, if she were given the responsibility of looking after us. Succumbing to an instinct of Polonius-like moral truisms, Grandpa reminded his son that however bad things get, others are always worse off, "especially in wartime."

He had an inarguable point, but the Muehlebach compromise trumped it. What made it work was my dad's decision to give up his Omaha pulpit and move his base to New York. He would accept a short-term but important assignment from the Zionists that had been on offer for months. That assignment entailed campaigning across the country as he had been doing during the summer. Omaha was therefore eliminated as a possible refuge for the waifs his two boys were fast becoming. But since my dad's assignment was supposed to be short-term, lasting only a year or so, and since he'd have an office in New York that he'd use as he orbited through, he could pledge that he'd regularly be on hand and would strive to reassemble his family as soon as possible. Our future would turn on whatever his next job would be, in whatever place. And so the arrangement for the children would have to last, like so many wartime arrangements, for what was called "the duration." The context had subtly changed. What kept our family scattered would no longer be my mom's impulsiveness and need but my dad's commitment, his larger purpose.

Or so it could be said. It was all very murky but my grandpa's argument had been effectively turned around. Besides, now that his only child was a rabbi, Grandpa had become an increasingly self-conscious Jew. A native New Yorker, Grandpa was the only child

himself of a London-born cigar maker whose namesake I am. "Joe Lelyveld Maker of Havana Cigars," my great-grandfather's shop-window on Madison Avenue and 117th Street had proclaimed. Joe's father, who came from Rotterdam bearing the Dutch name the family had acquired, became a chorister in a synagogue in London's East End. But when Joe crossed the Atlantic, he seems to have left whatever religion he had behind. Grandpa had long ago forbidden his little son to bring a blue-and-white Zionist flag into his home. "We'll have only one flag in this house, the American flag," he had said then, in my dad's rendition. But now he had to be proud that this same son was on an important mission for his people.

The mission was to end the schism among American Jews over the cause of building a Jewish national state in Palestine, then still under British control. My dad's job, as director of a new Zionist outfit called the Committee on Unity for Palestine, was to stump from one major Jewish community to the next, converting anti-Zionists and winning over those who had yet to commit themselves. A powerful platform speaker, a winning young man without sanctimonious rabbinic airs, he was well cast in the role. (A "1945-model Zionist leader, very blond, good-looking and American-boyish," a Jewish paper in San Francisco would gush.) From the perspective of a time in which most American Jews are anything but diffident in expressing support for whatever government sits in Jerusalem, pursuing whatever policy, aggressive or conciliatory, it's not easy to grasp the way in which a war that had been an unthinkable and absolute catastrophe for European Jewry deepened the schism among Jews in this country. But the militancy of anti-Zionists among American Jews, as well as the militancy of Zionists, was actually on the rise at the time my father decided to leave Omaha. In 1942, in what was for Americans the first summer of the war, a considerable rump of ninety Reform rabbis had gathered in Atlantic City to sign a manifesto opposing the nationalist program "in the light of our universalistic interpretation of Jewish history and endeavor." They did not, they said, want "to confuse our fellow men about our place and function in society." In other words, they did not want to be thought of as less American than any other community of believers; the war against Hitler was for all men, not Jews in particular. My dad's most cherished teachers from Hebrew Union College had signed the declaration, including my godfather, a benign elder with a white Vandyke beard named David Philipson, who gave the keynote address in Atlantic City. "The outlook of Reform Judaism is the world," he said. "The outlook of Zionism is a corner of Western Asia." My godfather was simply being true to the founding vision of Reform Judaism in America. The movement had specifically renounced national aspirations for the Jewish people in 1885, a dozen years before the Zionists first proclaimed themselves a movement. "We consider ourselves no longer a nation, but a religious community, and therefore expect neither a return to Palestine," the Reform platform had declared, "nor sacrificial worship under the sons of Aaron."

My father had trained in that tradition but Hitler's demolition of Germany's proud and assimilationist Jewish community in less than a decade had put him on the other side. He wrote vehement protest letters to senior rabbis a generation older and eagerly put his name to a Zionist counterdeclaration signed by 757 rabbis, 214 of them from the Reform camp. Two years later, words like "Auschwitz" and "Holocaust" still were not in use, and "genocide" was a term that had not even been coined, but the only question left about the destruction of Europe's Jews was how thorough it would prove to have been. The anti-Zionists argued it would be easier to place Jewish survivors if they were seen as having a claim on citizenship in all democratic lands rather than one. The American Council for Judaism, an anti-Zionist front that came into being in 1943 with behind-the-scenes backing from Arthur Hays Sulzberger, the publisher of *The New York Times*, said it hoped Palestine would be one of those lands;

that is, a multinational democracy "in which our fellow Jews shall be free Palestinians whose religion is Judaism, even as we are Americans whose religion is Judaism." The Zionists said that was delusional, that after the Nazis and the hard-heartedness of the West at a time when many lives could still have been saved, no self-respecting Jew could again doubt the need for a homeland.

My father had dreamed of going to China and North Africa, of engaging in projects of postwar reconstruction. Here was a cause even closer to his heart that would also come to a head at the end of the war. So a logic for his abrupt departure from Omaha can be easily traced, leaving only the question of whether it was his Zionism or his pursuit of my mom that actually set him in motion. It's a question that needn't be answered and that's unanswerable anyway in any definitive sense, but since a small piece of my life was left hanging in the balance, I'm moved to try. The timing, I'm tempted to say, shows that he gave himself full-time to the Zionist cause for love; or, putting it only slightly differently, that his motives were noble and very mixed. But it could also be, I have to acknowledge, that the looming prospect of finding himself in Omaha in a big house with a housekeeper and two small sons was hardly more appealing to him than his idea of sending us to Brooklyn had been to his dad. (If there was a worse idea, it was one that occurred to my mom. Not yet in psychoanalysis, she had actually suggested at one point that her mother come out to Omaha to live with my dad while she moved in with her father in Washington Heights.)

Even if my dad did it for love, none of this was at all apparent to me in Brooklyn, where weeks and later months could pass between visits by my parents and where, as far as I can remember, they never once appeared together the whole time I was there. What was apparent was the unfathomable change in my life. Becoming a New Yorker turned out to be tougher than becoming an Adventist in Tekamah. On the farm, I'd always known that the summer would eventually end. In Brooklyn there was no obvious limit, no sense of anything happening next. The future was soupy fog and more fog. My grandparents weren't keeping anything from me. They had no idea either about when they could expect relief. For me that blankness meant I'd have to get used to the strange and unnatural setting of the place, its brick-and-mortar density, the relentless march of streets blocking any horizon, the loud voices, with accents and inflections that seemed to screech in my ears.

Yet some things were obviously easier. I could finally be Joe, not Jo. I was far from being the solitary Jew in my class and I no longer stood out as "the rabbi's son." Where I was sent to Sunday school, the rabbi was a stranger, a remote figure with no more than a polite interest in me. I could also now buy war stamps at school like other kids, instead of peace stamps. My grandpa, who read the *Daily Mirror*, the jingoist tabloid that carried Walter Winchell's column, was no pacifist. (And though they were beyond my understanding, the views of my absent dad were probably evolving too. A commitment to nonviolence had no conspicuous place in the Zionist ethos he was now promoting.)

My grandpa was a hosiery salesman who could not go on the road because of wartime gas rationing. At his age—he was about to turn sixty—that meant he was washed up. If Arthur Miller hadn't had the prototype of Willy Loman in his own family, he could have based the character on Ed Lelyveld, a man who had once been dashing in his world but who now was more often dour as he sensed his life closing in on him. His 1941 Buick had been new when the war started, but now that it was impossible for him to use it to go calling on clients in Pennsylvania, Ohio, Indiana, and upstate New York, he had no commissions to rake in, only a meager base pay for time served in an office. By 1944 he might have had some foreboding but couldn't have yet imagined that he'd never be able to afford a trade-in for a new car after peace returned. When he died in my freshman year of college in 1955, the rusted-out Buick would still be parked on Ocean Parkway, a monument to his decline.

Grandpa was responsible for the distinctive decor of the apartment where I slept on a cot in the living room (unless one or both of my grandparents had a card game going, in which case I'd be put to sleep on a chaise in the corner of their bedroom where later in the night I'd be roused by their huge snores). His decorative touches included a collection of still lifes he'd painted before packing away his brushes at the age of eighteen or nineteen and the fishing rods he left standing in unreeled coils of line in three of the living room's four corners. Every Saturday, except in the frigid dead of winter, he would drive to Sheepshead Bay or Freeport and spend the day at the rail of a fishing boat, returning in the evening with flounder or bluefish or porgies. After letting down his suspenders so they dangled around his knees and putting on reading glasses, he would then clean his catch at the kitchen sink.

Sometimes Grandpa lost his temper in ways my dad never had. I never got over being startled by his explosions, which came unpredictably. I can even remember him undoing his belt buckle, which he wore on the left side of his not insubstantial paunch, as if he were about to remove the belt and whack me. On one or two occasions, the belt came all the way off but I don't think I ever got hit. As he went into his windup, Grandma would step between us, shouting. They would then argue at the tops of their voices and I'd escape. In the apartment house on Ocean Parkway, escape was easy night or day. The place was a vertical village with two elevators, front and back, and the apartments of my friends were seldom closed to me. Before long I knew the names of most of the tenants and they knew mine. It was hardly ever difficult to round up a few kids to romp through the basement or, weather permitting, hang out outside.

One such occasion stands out as it would for anyone of my generation. A week after my eighth birthday, I was listening to one of my late afternoon radio serials—I'm fairly sure it was *Superman* or *Captain Midnight* but I've heard others contend that it had to have been *Tom Mix*—when an announcer broke in with a bulletin: President Roosevelt was dead of a cerebral hemorrhage. The station then played solemn music without any indication that my program would return. Grandma was standing at the stove in the little kitchen alcove when I told her. Weeping, screaming, still holding her frying pan, she bolted across the hall to deliver the news to her neighbor Mollie Steinberg, who shrieked into the phone she had been holding, then dropped the receiver. Struck by the clamor of their responses, I ran downstairs to collect some friends. We all then raced to the foot of the steps at Avenue P and McDonald Avenue where the subway, in the confusing argot of New York, was an "elevated." There most of the men in the neighborhood would be returning from work in what Brooklynites still call "the city."

"President Roosevelt is dead, President Roosevelt is dead," we chirped at each new batch of office workers that came down the stairs. To a man—and to a woman also, I suppose, if there were any—they were visibly thunderstruck. It was my first and most immediate experience of delivering the news. The same batch of kids would go to the movies most Saturday afternoons at the Claridge Theater, also on Avenue P, where we would sit through black-and-white double features, racing noisily to the men's room whenever they got too scary, ignoring the shushing of the white-gowned "matron" who was supposed to keep juveniles in order. I can't identify the movie but one such seat-emptying episode sticks in my head. A fine upstanding American man and a fine upstanding American woman were being tortured by enemy infiltrators in the basement of a house in what I took to be San Francisco. The possibility that enemies had infiltrated Brooklyn then lodged in our minds. We saw some conduct in the neighborhood that struck us as a little suspicious—such as a man we didn't recognize in a double-parked car we'd never seen—just as I sometimes imagined I'd glimpsed the periscope of a German U-boat among the whitecaps in the Narrows as my grandpa drove on the Belt Parkway. But we never could be sure.

My mom's determination not to see me came under early assault from her own father. Izzy Bookholtz, an expert tool-and-die maker and dreamy inventor of gadgets in which no one ever invested, had lived in Salem, Massachusetts, after leaving Warsaw, then moved to New York, where he met Gussie Sonberg, from Lodz by way of Radom, who became my grandma. When Gussie was a little girl her father managed a large estate and she had a governess. Her family fell on hard times but her early experience of privilege left her with a keen sense of social status that expressed itself in contradictory ways. As a teenager she briefly got in trouble in Radom for passing out socialist leaflets. Later, as a recently certified American, she badgered Izzy into putting away his tools and becoming an insurance agent so he could leave for work in a respectable suit and tie. My mom's mom drove everyone hard, herself most of all, working as a seamstress in union shops in the garment district until she was nearly seventy and polishing the drainpipe under her kitchen sink till it gleamed like family silver. The set of her mouth, the tone of her voice, were enough to tell her eldest daughter when she was falling short of Grandma's high expectations. That happened often, but Gussie Bookholtz always found mitigating factors when one of her grandchildren transgressed. "He meant well," she'd invariably say, extending a mercy, a little slack, my mom could have used. Grandpa B—as we called him to distinguish him from Grandpa L—broke down and wept when telling my mother that he hadn't known how to reply when her son called and asked for her. "I can't talk with Jo," she wrote my dad. "I don't know how to answer his questions."

The pressure, much of it self-generated, only mounts. Soon she is writing in pleading tones, begging my dad to "step in and take over what I should never have dropped." Her handwriting actually changes; it wanders and trails off. Her sweetly mild and sometimes timid father has become "inconsolable" on the issue. So has she. "We must find someone who *wants* to take care of Jo," she writes. The word "wants" is underscored twice. I stare at it now in sadness for her but also with a touch of sullen pride. Very tentatively but surely, I know, that "someone" was already being felt in my life. Joe was discovering that he could "take care of Jo."

Finally, having put the problem before her new psychiatrist, who tells her it's all right for her to see me, she comes to Brooklyn one evening unannounced. I cry for what my grandma says was the first time since I've been there. Suddenly, in my mom's account, I'm "tense, demanding and not the boy Mother L knows." Most disturbing to her, I'm "full of plans" about coming to live with her, which she then has to forestall. She explains that she goes to school; I say so do I. She says she isn't home at lunchtime; I say I could eat at the drugstore soda fountain. She says she also gets home late; I say I could play in the street. My mother, who was then living in a rented room on West 111th Street where she shared the bathroom and kitchen with other tenants, concludes that I have "many troubles." She hopes, she writes to my dad, that "they aren't too much for him."

Her visit wasn't soon repeated. My dad's unheralded appearances, at dinnertime scarcely once a month, were almost as infrequent. I sometimes wondered where he lived. If he was in New York, it was usually the old Commodore Hotel. I've the dimmest memory of having glimpsed the studio apartment my mom eventually rented that autumn in a townhouse on West 113th Street. But I don't think I ever stayed there overnight. My only clear memory of seeing her in the Brooklyn apartment was in early winter when I was laid up on the living room sofa with chicken pox. That time she came for a whole afternoon. Another visitor was there too, a woman who asked me a nosy leading question about how long I'd be staying in Brooklyn. I responded by announcing, "My parents are divorced."

I doubt that anything I'd ever said before in my life had produced an impact on adults equal to what I then witnessed. My grandma, who was given to stagy exclamations, gasped audibly and demanded to know who'd told me that. She seemed to suspect I knew something she didn't. Otherwise Dora Lelyveld would have said, "Ah, go on," her usual expression when she thought someone was fooling or exaggerating. My mom, blushing and looking flustered as everyone stared her way, declared that I didn't know what the word meant. Maybe I didn't but my bold assertion had really been a question about how things stood between my parents. I got no answer that afternoon. On another occasion, I found my grandma red-eyed from weeping. She said it was all over between my parents. To me that simply confirmed that I wouldn't be coming up for parole anytime soon.

It was another few months before I next saw my mom. That was on my first and last visit to her in a part of Queens known as Bellerose, where she was confined to a private psychiatric hospital for four months after the most serious of the several breakdowns she would have in a long and eventually tranquil life. It happened around the turn of 1945. My dad, who had positioned himself to be nearby if she wanted or needed him, was there to pick up the pieces. But once she was in the hospital in Bellerose, she was placed under a no-visitors ban in the early weeks, and that ban included—that's to say excluded—him. So again, as he stumped his way to the West Coast for the Zionists at the start of a tour that was to last two months, stopping in Omaha, Denver, and Salt Lake City on his way to San Francisco, the daily letters started. She had implored him to write. The previous summer his tone had been injured and long-suffering, deliberately cool. Now it was again ardent, full of hope and cheer as if that was what the doctor had prescribed. It also became apparent that my dad had his own need to seize on hope.

The fact that she wanted to hear from him had "lifted the heaviest of the weights lying on my heart," he wrote in one of the first of these daily letters. "I need you just as much as you need me," he was writing a few days later in a letter that became surprisingly confessional. "I never realized before how central in my life and activities was the effort to meet your standards—and when I thought you didn't care, the impetus, the ambition and everything else fell away." Without her he had lapsed into a dismal "self-concern—a paramount need to prove to myself that I was not without virility and attractiveness for the opposite sex." Whether he knew or suspected that she might have become involved with someone else, his intention here seemed to have less to do with unburdening himself than granting a fragile, hospitalized mate a form of connubial absolution, assuring her that whatever was past would now be past forever.

"We're going to build much happiness," he writes from the Hotel Sir Francis Drake in San Francisco, "for ourselves and for Jo and Davy." It's the first time we're explicitly included in any vision of the future.

I've a memory of the drive to Bellerose to see my mom in the hospital. The occasion was a visit from an Omaha scrap metals dealer whose brother and sister-in-law had become close friends of our family. The visitor, whose name was Sam Ferer, was less well known to me. He arrived in a black limousine with a driver, wearing a suntan and a gray coat with a black velvet collar. His silver hair was combed straight back and his manner stayed cheerful from start to finish, as if he were the leader on a holiday outing. As I now picture it, Sam sat in the front on the way out to Queens, with Grandpa, Grandma, and me in the rear and David, presumably, on someone's lap. Or did Grandma stay home? The picture tends to blur around the edges but I see a brick structure on fenced grounds, with a circular driveway and my mom in slacks and a flannel shirt. Her hair is different, loosely drawn back. Her manner has also changed. She is tentative, a little shy, a little tearful, surprisingly tender. When I think of that afternoon, I realize how unused I'd become over the years to being hugged by my mother. The visit does not last long but she promises to see us soon. My mom wasn't happy to be put on show for Sam Ferer, but within a few days she writes to my dad to suggest that she find an apartment in time for his return from his tour so that we could all have a family Passover together.

My dad, presumably guided by her doctors, with whom he consults weekly, thinks this is "rushing things." His letters from California have been chatty, elated accounts of the headway he has made winning over supporters of the American Council for Judaism, the anti-Zionist faction, spiced up with heady gossip about dinner at the Brown Derby with a screenwriter friend, encounters with Eddie Cantor and Paul Robeson, glimpses of Harpo Marx and Fred Astaire. Now, writing from San Antonio as he heads back East, he suggests that they wait till the fall before involving the kids in their own eventual reunion. "I don't want you plunging into the responsibilities of housekeeping and the children all at once," he writes. "Let's you and I try it alone for a while. I want you for myself . . ." It's June before they're together again, for the first time in a year, in a borrowed apartment of a friend, a small penthouse on West 84th Street. And it's September before I arrive, after another summer in camp followed by a visit to cousins in Massachusetts who smarten me up for my big homecoming by putting me in a new outfit featuring brown-and-white saddle shoes, a sporty tweed jacket, and a clip-on bow tie. So that's how I was sent home to my parents, wherever home would prove to be—gift-wrapped. It hadn't been the war that had scattered our family, but it seemed right, nonetheless, that our reunion coincided with the Japanese surrender in Tokyo Bay. I could now believe that peace would change our lives.

My homecoming actually brought me to the borrowed penthouse. On my first night under the same roof as my parents in fifteen months, a peek into the living room sent me to sleep with a warm

feeling of contentment I can still summon. I'd wakened an hour or two after being put to bed and tiptoed out of my room, drawn by a light I could see through a crack in the door. Once I got to the threshold of the living room, I saw my parents embracing and kissing on the couch. It was possible to reach the advanced age of eight in that era, as it probably isn't now in an age of cable TV and the Internet, without ever having heard of what grown-ups do together. Anyhow, I hadn't (and wouldn't for yet another year). But after taking in the scene for an instant, I tiptoed back to bed without having been noticed, all too easily convinced that I finally had the answer to the question of how things stood between my parents. In later years, I'd think of that scene when things started to go sour again. To it I probably owe a substantial portion of my exaggerated faith in romantic love as a cure for every ailment and affliction.

In a week or two we moved into an apartment on Riverside

Drive in a building that stood just in front of the townhouse where my mom had suffered her crack-up eight months earlier. The apartment had a broad view of the Palisades across the Hudson; at night you could see the lights on the roller coaster at the old amusement park and neon signs on top of the shoreline plants of Ford and Spry, a vegetable shortening used in baking. The Spry sign spelled out the name, s-p-r-y, then blinked; the Ford sign, as I recall it, just blinked.

For the rest of her life, my mother loved telling the story of how we grabbed the apartment at a time of acute shortage, when family housing was not to be found in Manhattan. (Late in life, fixated on this period, she even attempted to set it down on paper as a short story.) She had seen a classified ad in the *Times* with a phone number and advice to call at the end of the long Labor Day weekend. No address was given. Determined to steal a march on the legions of other apartment hunters, she sat down to read the Manhattan phone directory, page by page and column by column, with the aim of locating the building by finding that single phone number, a needle in a stack of digits. After two days she was bleary-eyed and only on the C's or D's, constantly going back to reread columns of numbers for fear her concentration had lapsed. A Cincinnati friend then showed up, called information, and asked to speak to the supervisor, for whom he brazenly spun a heartbreaking tale of an elderly aunt who was not picking up the phone and whose address he had lost while serving in the Pacific. It could be a matter of life and death, he kept telling the supervisor. The con worked. When the tenants returned from their weekend, my mother was camped on the doorstep.

The building had seen better days. This we learned from the elevator operators, two light-skinned Negroes—that was the term then—named Henderson and Walker who were not called Mister or by their first names, even by children. The one exception was Grandma B, who unfailingly said, "Good afternoon, Mr. Walker," or "Good evening, Mr. Henderson." The elevator men, whose jobs were eventually terminated with the installation of a self-service elevator, remembered when Al Jolson kept a mistress on the second floor whom he visited most afternoons. Now the building was half full of Columbia graduate students and assorted Bartlebys from Manhattan offices who rented rooms in apartments controlled by Mrs. Nelson, an ill-kempt harridan who went from floor to floor in a housedress to collect overdue rents. More than anything else, I wanted to believe in the cohesion and stability of my family. But the notion that we were finally settled didn't sink in for a couple of years, until one Yom Kippur morning when workers arrived with sledgehammers to knock down the wall to the next apartment, into which we were about to expand. I then got a room of my own, which meant that the tyranny I'd imposed on my brother while we shared a room could now be eased.

In October 1945, a month after we moved into the apartment, the U.S. Navy lined up its carriers, battleships, and destroyers, forty-eight of them, along a seven-mile stretch of the Hudson in a final victory parade before they went into mothballs. Each ship fired off a twenty-one-gun salute as President Truman cruised by. I felt the reverberations on my forehead, which I pressed to our living room window. It seemed amazing that I'd gotten that close to a president, but eight months later I felt even closer when I learned that my own father had actually got to sit and talk with him in his office at the White House.

The White House visit at the end of June 1946 was one of my dad's last missions as a full-time Zionist organizer. His fight against Jewish anti-Zionists had turned into a rout, thanks in some measure to his persuasion of Jewish elites in city after city. But it was, finally, the pictures from the Nazi death camps that all but ended the debate among American Jews: the piles of skeletons, the bins of hair and teeth. A Roper poll in the fall of 1945 showed that support for the anti-Zionist position among American Jews had dwindled to 10 percent. The anti-Zionists still had the ear of the State Department, however, so everything depended on the new president, whose initial support for a Jewish homeland was being tested by the contrary advice he was getting from officials and by a reflexive backlash inside himself against too much Jewish pressure. In plain language, Harry Truman as much as said that he was sick and tired of being lectured to by rabbis. ("Jesus Christ couldn't please them when he was on earth," he said.) But my dad, then only thirty-three, got into the Oval Office on the coattails of Eddie Jacobson, Truman's old partner in a Kansas City haberdashery. Also along was an executive of a shirt company named Kaplan. "Kaplan sells shirts, I sell furnishings," Jacobson told reporters when they emerged, "and the Rabbi sells notions." My dad came home thinking he had made a sale but the argument continued to rage in the Truman administration until, finally, the president recognized the new state of Israel two years later, in May 1948.

The fact that we returned from camp in the summer of 1946 to the same home from which we'd set out was a kind of milestone. This hadn't happened in four years. It was also the autumn I became a sports nut, at about the moment that Enos Slaughter won the World Series for the St. Louis Cardinals by sprinting from first base to home on a single. I was then inspired to read the first book supposedly for grown-ups I ever managed to finish. It was an autographed copy of *Lucky to Be a Yankee* by Joe DiMaggio and it became the foundation of a baseball library of thirty or forty books, including books on how to play various infield and outfield positions that I was to discover, after much trying, I'd never be able to manage with any confidence or flair.

No other kid at P.S. 165 had Truman's *and* DiMaggio's autographs. I think of that nine-year-old who was once me and shudder to see how hard he was having to work to define himself as someone special. Was that because he felt himself to be different from his newest set of friends, or because he needed to be different? Was be-

ing different himself a way of explaining why his parents seemed to
lead lives that were so different from the lives of the parents of his
friends? He labors to make a plus out of the fact that he sees so little
of them. He doesn't see them, obviously, because they're busy and
important people. In his new job at Hillel, his father is still often on
the road, for ten days or two weeks at a shot. His mother, who has
become a Hillel Foundation director at Hunter College herself
while completing her dissertation, comes home well after his dinner
most evenings. Her psychoanalysis has ended abruptly with the disappearance one day of the analyst, who was found after a while, a
suicide. (Later my dad would say that the doctor had fallen in love
with his patient. As far as I know, my mother never again put her
faith in a therapist.) Our household is kept going by two maids in
tandem, each named Dorothy. Once he has his own room, this ten-
year-old me is reclusive there, listening to ballgames on the radio or
reading. Of course, I now forget more than I remember, but I think
that boy is too solemn, too responsible, too self-absorbed. I doubt
he has much fun. I know he would disagree, that he would not be
able to say what's missing in his life, but still to me, from this great
distance, he seems too lonely, too singular.

"You've got to be more outgoing," his dad, who found him puzzling, would advise. His usual response was silence. Or did that
happen later, when he was a fully fledged adolescent? Whenever it
was, I recall that it happened a lot. (Of course, if I think about it
now, I realize that a lot could mean three times.) Telling him to be
outgoing was as helpful as commanding someone to be funny or
spontaneous. It promoted a sense of life as a continuing audition
that left him nonplussed. Now there's an adjective, nonplussed, that
I could do without. I don't like its Latinate fussiness. But it seems
right in this context, for it describes being brought to a state in
which one is unable to proceed in speech or action. The O.E.D. offers a rare and ponderous noun, *nonplussation*: the act of putting

another in that state, the condition of being in it. Nonplussation is what we regularly did to one another, my dad and I, but not without love and a pained look in his eyes that had to have been reflected in mine.

Three memories stand out as more than a little telling. They float in time, in no particular order, with months or years, for all I know, between them. Each involves "him," this elusive, earlier me, asking a tricky question of his mother. It was a time in his life when he brooded much on the universal prospect of annihilation and death, a preoccupation that was especially likely to seize him, for some reason, on rainy days when he rode on the upper deck of one of the old double-decker buses of the Fifth Avenue Coach Company to and from piano lessons or Sunday school. If the God they talked about there allowed us to be erased, turned to dust, why were we supposed to be so grateful? For a rabbi's son, this issue raised epistemological questions not only about the cosmic order but about his father's understanding of it.

One of the questions asked of his mother, therefore, was whether she believed in the hereafter. She searched his face, as if trying to see what might be behind this sudden outburst, these intimations of mortality. Then she replied with great deliberation, "I believe that man can make heaven on earth." (In other words, no; or, take some of what you hear in synagogues with a grain of salt.) The next question was whether his father was a great man. This time she seemed to be replying positively but then hedged, saying something like this: "Yes, I think he *could* be a great man." (In other words, maybe but probably not.) Finally he asked the meaning of the word "masturbation," which he'd found in a magazine for men, not boys, that he'd bought because it had a ballplayer on the cover. He assumed the word was synonymous with sex, the incredible, inevitable mechanics of which he now thought he understood. He understood them, of course, the way a deaf person understands Mozart, but he wanted to hear what she'd say. The answer must have been evasive, or so involved as to be over his head, or something he needed to repress very fast. It's significant, I'm sure, that I've no recollection of her answer at all. (In other words, ask your father.)

What was still probably for this distant me the larger question of how things stood between his parents had not really been answered by the family's reunion or settling in on Riverside Drive. I had simply stopped asking. There were warning signs once I was old enough to interpret them. The most obvious was that my parents slept toe to toe on adjacent studio couches (because of Dad's snoring, so Mom said). Then there were the times my mom seemed tense or very low, either unreachable or full of loud complaints—about my grandparents, money, or hypocrisies of various kinds, which she was always quick, often too quick, to spot. When she was in that state, she could sound scornful for minutes at a time, ending usually with an exit to another room. The scorn didn't attach to her children, but if my dad took slight exception to the drift of what she'd been saying, he would find that he was not immune.

My mother and I did more to set the tone of moodiness in our household than my dad and brother. I'd have considered our way of being normal had it not been for a contrasting period of ease, approaching harmony, lasting nearly a year that I date from the end of the summer of 1947. I was then ten and David six. We arrived from Maine at Pennsylvania Station—the real McKim, Mead & White Penn Station, not the underground circle of hell that has existed since its razing—and were taken up the grand marble staircase to a coffee shop at the top, on the left. In my memory, early morning summer sunlight slants across the high-ceilinged space. And there, once our oatmeal and raisin toast have been ordered, our parents tell us we will soon have a little brother or sister. They cannot contain their excitement, their joy. They're not looking away from each other but at each other. I would never see them happier. Whatever is in the air, I want to bottle and preserve it. And I feel the sense of contentment, which maybe translates as safety, that I'd felt in the borrowed penthouse two years earlier. At the least, I've been given a lesson in resilience.

The birth of my youngest brother, Michael, came at the end of February on a day so unseasonably balmy that I'd taken my baseball mitt out of winter storage in my closet where it had been duly slathered with neat's-foot oil and tied up with a ball since the autumn. As the light faded and I wound up the season's first catch with a pal in the park, I saw my dad coming down the hill from Broadway, beaming with the news that would throw our normally tense household into a state approaching bliss.

Michael was fortunate to make it home from the hospital as a complete male child. At his *bris*, the ritual that traditionally accompanies the circumcision of a son, my infant brother was held in the lap of his godfather, Stephen S. Wise, the great rabbinic figure of an era then ending. Wise, who had scarcely a year to live, was already frail and bent; his skin drawn close across his skull looked drained of color to the point of translucence, more like parchment than flesh. The sight of the aging rabbi, dressed in his habitual black suit, so startled the doctor who was to snip off Michael's foreskin that his hand started to shake. Later the doctor explained that Rabbi Wise had officiated at a wedding that had been the prologue to a catastrophic marriage he'd since done his best to forget. Traumatized, the doctor failed to make a neat slice; there was more blood than usual but no permanent damage done. Stephen Wise referred to "the savage and bloody rites" in a letter he then addressed to the infant, announcing that Michael would soon be receiving a silver kiddush cup with the inscription "To Mike From Steve." The wry demotic touch was so conspicuously out of character—it may have been the first and last time Stephen Wise was referred to as Steve by himself or anyone—that it came across as a singular expression of affection for its recipient and his family.

The newcomer had dark hair and large mesmerizing brown eyes. The other males in the family had fair hair and blue eyes. My mother's eyes were greenish but everyone said Michael took after her side; as one of a kind, he was even more prized. Our baby brother would continue to be doted on but the bliss he bestowed on the household proved to be transient. When I returned from camp at the end of the summer of 1948, I found my mom once again picking fights with my dad, repeatedly voicing her suspicion that he was attracted to a woman in his office whom she dismissed as "common." My dad's exasperated denials, aimed at closing the subject once and for all, got him nowhere.

How my recollection of these years turns on those last days of summer, that fortnight of transition when, it seemed, almost anything could happen. I had an opportunity to study the alleged temptress as I cruised up the Hudson with my parents on the open upper deck of a riverboat, one of the fleet of old steamers known as Dayliners. We were on our way with a large group of students and rabbis drawn from campuses across the country to a Hillel retreat near Kingston. The woman was wearing tight white shorts with platform shoes and very red lipstick. My ideas of what made a woman enticing had to be largely derivative. Pre-adolescent still, I found it preposterous that my mother could feel a tiny bit jealous of a woman who looked older and fleshier; friendly perhaps but utterly lacking her own taut beauty.

In 1948 there were weightier subjects to think about. Babe Ruth had just died of throat cancer, less than three months after I'd gone to Yankee Stadium for his last appearance there on what was called Babe Ruth Day. The Cleveland Indians under Lou Boudreau, whose book *Good Infield Play* had made me only slightly less mediocre, seemed destined to vanquish my Yankees. And for the first time, I was aware of a presidential election. Harry Truman, whose autograph I had, was a hopeless underdog, everyone said. Because he had kept his pledge to recognize the new state of Israel, he had the

NOT FROM THIS PLACE | 81

gratitude and support of most Jews. But not my dad's. There had been too much backtracking on the road to recognition, including an American plan for a trusteeship in Palestine that might have precluded a Jewish homeland. Then, after recognition, Truman was unresponsive to Zionist pleas that he ease an embargo on arms for the suddenly besieged state. The former pacifist felt that after his conversation with the president two years earlier, Israel might have expected something other than the cold shoulder it was now receiving from a Washington eager to rebuild the bridges to the Arabs it had just burned.

So my dad was supporting Henry Wallace, which meant I was too, although I couldn't have said why. An Iowa farmer and former vice president who would have briefly succeeded President Roosevelt had he died only a few months earlier, Wallace was running as the candidate of a newly proclaimed Progressive Party that had Communists and what were called fellow travelers in most of its key positions. I wouldn't have grasped that then, but my dad did. He'd had an argumentative lunch with a college buddy, Arnold Beichman, his successor at the *Columbia Spectator*, the man whose penthouse we'd borrowed for our family reunion. A newspaperman, Arnold put anti-Communism on a par with anti-Fascism as a moral cause: a position that, bless his soul, he's still ready to argue with passion in his nineties. Arnold remembered as a turning point in his own political education my dad's rejection of an article he'd written as an undergraduate for being naïve about blatant Communist propaganda. He couldn't believe that religion had turned his formerly tough-minded editor into what the Hearst papers would have called a Commie dupe.

Not so. My dad seldom mixed socially with old college friends who'd become Communists. Only when they'd renounced their faith would we see them on anything approaching a regular basis. Once when I complained to him that I didn't see why I had to go to school on my birthday, he did say, "Joseph Stalin goes to work on his birthday." But that must have been nothing more than aberrant thought association, remembered by me only because it was the first time I'd ever heard of Joseph Stalin. (Years later when I reminded him of this remark, he thought it impossible that he could ever have said any such thing. Except for the fact that the memory boy knew he couldn't have made it up, I had to agree.) My dad was fundamentally not a political man. Sore as he was at Truman over his wobbles on Palestine, he simply did not want to hear that Henry Wallace was a dupe, not the Henry Wallace who'd actually traveled to the Promised Land, where his cultivator's soul had been stirred by the sight of carrots growing in the Negev; not the Henry Wallace who'd given a well-known World War II homily on "the Century of the Common Man" that opened with an appeal to the prophetic vision of social justice in the Old Testament and closed with a passage from Isaiah (*He giveth power to the faint; and to them that have no might he increaseth strength*). A man whose vision was rooted in the soil and the prophets had to be a respectable recipient of a protest vote in an election that was sure to be won, anyway, by the Republican, Thomas Dewey.

I knew "The Century of the Common Man" only as a calypso song on a record my dad had picked up. It was sung by a Trinidadian singer named Sir Lancelot who actually lived in Los Angeles (where, I now discover from a record liner, he broke into movies as the Caribbean crewmate of Humphrey Bogart in *To Have and Have Not*). Heard today, his song can make you nostalgic for a time when Americans were thought to be on the side of the world's downtrodden. It still wears better than the speech:

> *Let the Fascists talk about the Superior Race,*
> *It will lead them to de-feat and disgrace;*
> *Americans have the superior plan,*
> *They're going to make this the Century of the Common Man . . .*

I had no idea that Sir Lancelot had been inspired by Henry Wallace, who began his pilgrimage as a Republican and would end, after falling out of the embrace of Communists, by backing a Republican, Dwight Eisenhower, for president, a job he thought he should have had himself.

On the Hudson River Dayliner at the end of that summer of 1948, there was one person who was prepared to hear out my views on the Cleveland Indians, Babe Ruth, and presidential politics (putting my preoccupations of that time in what I would have felt was a descending order of importance). That was Ben Lowell. I met him there on that upper deck for the first time. I picture him in white slacks, but that could be memory's creative costuming, drawn from some subsequent outing. What I know for sure is that by the time we reached Kingston, I felt we were on our way to becoming fast friends.

4

B E N

So Ben, now it's your turn, time to fill in the gaps in the lost narrative of your life. Those gaps were part of what made you an intriguing figure, if not a figure of intrigue, in the years my younger self learned to rely on your friendship. How you found your way from an Alabama pulpit to Hollywood and what you actually did there were stories you told only in bits and pieces. Did you become a film editor or were you involved in marketing? I never got it straight. You said you strained your eyes in cutting rooms, reviewed pictures before they were released, and went to sneak previews to gauge audience reactions. Did you mix with stars? You never said you did, never said you didn't. You spoke knowingly of various jobs and specialties in the business, dropped a few low-wattage names and left it at that.

When I thought about what I knew about you after you disappeared from my life, I had to admit you'd been a little elusive. But when you were there, you were a solid presence, always self-assured, apparently never conflicted. Adults described you as "magnetic." Decades later, they would still recall you as "a charmer." Yet they experienced you as transient, an asteroid passing through on its own fixed course. In a binary fission of your own devising, you managed to produce two rabbis, Goldstein and Lowell, from a single life and ordination. But, it turns out, they weren't enough. Actually you had three names, for on occasions in the thirties and forties, you found it expedient to introduce yourself as George B. Stern, using your first wife's maiden name. You dressed carefully and conservatively yet, unlike everyone else we knew, showed zero interest in possessions. In the three years you lived in New York after your Hollywood sojourn, you always resided in hotels: first the Gotham with your second wife, then the Henry Hudson on your own.

By the time you came back East, the FBI had been keeping a file on you for seven years. Not altogether implausibly, they thought you might be a Soviet agent. But whenever the FBI men assigned to Goldstein or Lowell tried to get a fix on you, they were soon reassigned to less speculative, more pressing cases and yours was put back on hold. Did you ever suspect that agents were logging your mail and phone calls and hanging out in the lobby of the building in Times Square where you and my dad worked? They were trying to pick you out of the crowd and establish a visual identification, a feat they were unable to accomplish after several tries, though you worked regular office hours every day. Not unlike ourselves, only much more so, they knew everything and nothing about you.

Only three scraps of paper survive tying me to you. One is an undated note from you accompanying a book you said I'd wanted. (If it wasn't a baseball book, it was most likely a book about mountaineering, my next obsession.) Another is a list of phone messages I left for my parents one evening when they were out and I was babysitting my brothers at below market rates. In its mock formality, one of the messages gleams with pride: "Benjamin B. Lowell called—for me." It's signed "J.L." All that's missing is a flourish of exclamation points. For *ME!!!* is what it unmistakably shouts. The final scrap of paper is a letter to my parents in the summer of 1949, carrying on a private joke from which they're excluded. "Tell Ben," it says, "to give my regards to Will Watsongassen. He'll understand." Now that I've finally traced your steps in Montgomery, I recognize that the suffix of that made-up name echoes the name of a

prominent Jewish family there, the Gassenheimers, which suggests
that the silly wordplay may have been as much yours as mine. Otherwise, though the reference is wholly opaque, irretrievable, it con-
veys the level of banter between us: low and corny. Having filled in
some of the gaps in my own early narrative, I don't find it hard now
to understand why your consistent and reliable interest in me came
to matter in my life.

So the questions that have lingered in my mind all these years,
Ben, are what force kept you on your peculiar trajectory and who
were you really? Such questions are ultimately unanswerable, of
course, in our own lives and those of the living who are close to us,
let alone someone so long gone. My memories gave me the strong
impulse to seek you out but carried no insight. The only traces of
your own memories would have to be found in scraps of correspondence, if any survived. Not only because I've no talent for fiction but
also because I wanted to know you, not create you, I had to resist
the idea that I might summon up, through an act of imagination,
your sense of your life, then lodge it in a fictional persona bearing
your name. So it was as a reporter and scavenger in archives that I
sought you. You're mentioned in passing in academic studies of the
Scottsboro case or southern Jews, but those references amount, at
best, to snapshots; you're caught in the flash of a moment, only to
disappear. The story of your life wasn't even known to your children. It may not always seem that way but I mean this exploration
as a kind of homage; that and, secondarily, as an attempt to round
out and perhaps put to rest an early chapter of my own life.

I found Ben's eldest and only surviving daughter, Josie, on a tidy
cul-de-sac of semiattached houses with little front porches, suggestive in a Disneyfied way of isolated prairie farmhouses. A one-street
development, it was actually on a bluff above an interstate in

Knoxville, Tennessee. I reached that street, following her directions, by driving through the parking lot of a vast ultramarine Wal-Mart on the far side of the highway. Josie, these days known to most of her friends as Jo, became my living link to Ben. Now nearing seventy, she moved with difficulty on arthritic legs as she led me into the ordered calm of her parlor. It may have been wish fulfillment but I thought at once that I could see Ben's open, winning expression reflected in the features of her broad face.

Josie was the daughter who once rode horses in Pennsylvania. She'd been placed in a boarding school there, she explained, after rebelling against having to go back to the elite private school where she'd been enrolled in New York. She was often rebellious in those years, which turn out to have been the years Ben was closest to me. Long after her parents divorced, Josie would refuse to go out with her dad when he came by on weekends in New York to see his daughters. She did this, she said, not to hurt him but to hurt her mother, a woman who was at once proud, querulous, and insecure but who retained a residual loyalty to her former husband that she wanted her daughters to share. Now Jo also allows that she was playing hard to get, that she wanted her father to try for her love more than he seemed able or ready to do. Once they divorced, her parents wanted to be called Margaret and Ben instead of Mom and Dad. Never did she hear Margaret blame Ben. Never did Margaret explain the divorce. Her mother's sister Elsie said once that it had happened because Margaret wouldn't buy into Ben's dream of moving the family to Russia. She didn't know whether that was ever literally Ben's plan, but it seems to her likely that her parents grew estranged over politics. Whether Margaret quarreled with Ben over another woman or simply failed to pass an ideological test is beyond anyone's knowing now. He divorced her in 1945 after they'd been married eighteen years and there was no contest.

Before she was nine, Josie's dad had already become a fleeting presence in her life, staying away for days at a time from the last home her parents shared, a spacious Craftsman's bungalow on South Wilton Place in Los Angeles purchased with funds her mother's mother had made available. The 1936 blue Packard in the driveway had been similarly acquired. On a couple of occasions, Ben Goldstein had loaned the Packard to officials of the Soviet consulate in Los Angeles, according to his FBI file. It was one of the things that kept the bureau interested in him. Once he was gone for good, Margaret Goldstein packed her daughters into the Packard and drove back to New York, where she resumed the use of her maiden name as soon as she heard of Ben's remarriage and subsequent name change. If he wasn't going to be a Goldstein, she saw no reason for her to remain one.

So when Ben Lowell later called on his daughters in New York, they were doubly removed from him as Josie and Linda Stern. Linda, the younger one who'd go out with Ben when Josie refused, always said she wouldn't marry a man with a name like Goldstein. Later she found herself married to a Goldberg. When that marriage ended, she didn't call herself Linda Stern again; she called herself Linda Benjamin, but by then the tribute to her dad was posthumous. Josie married an engineering student named Rogers and became Jo Rogers. Her husband's company, Magnavox, moved them to Tennessee, where they raised four children. John Rogers, who later perished driving his car off a highway, possibly after a drinking bout, was a lapsed Catholic who had tried Unitarianism. Only one of their four children now considers herself Jewish, but that's because her best friends when she was growing up in Tennessee were Jews, not because the grandfather she never met was a rabbi. From a parochial point of view, this can be seen as a story of assimilation. From the standpoint of the broader culture, it's a typical American story of the dispersal and flinging apart of families.

Jo Rogers is an independent, intellectually alert woman who

now says of her father, "I wish I'd known him." Yet on my two visits to Knoxville as she pulled out family pictures, documents, and her own disconnected memories, I felt myself reintroduced to the figure whom she remembers best for the emotional void he left behind. When she spoke about the end of the marriage as she experienced it, I could begin to imagine its start, which allowed me to glimpse Ben and Margaret Goldstein before they had their fateful collision in Alabama with a social order that prized conformity above all else, welcoming outsiders with its vaunted hospitality only so long as they didn't presume to meddle or judge.

As reflected in the one surviving picture of their wedding in Jo's possession, it had been a dignified and auspicious launch. The date is June 1, 1926. The location is the apartment of Josephine May Wise, Margaret's twice-widowed mother, in a then exclusive Seventh Avenue apartment house a couple of blocks down from Carnegie Hall. On the wedding certificate, the forceful signature of her brother-in-law, Stephen S. Wise, fills the space left for the officiator. Already the city's and probably the nation's most prominent rabbi, he's an orator likened to William Jennings Bryan, a Zionist from the days of Theodor Herzl, a civic reformer, social activist, and friend of statesmen starting with Woodrow Wilson. The bride is a stepdaughter of his late brother. Bride and groom stand in front of a lush bower of palm fronds laced with roses, peonies, and lilacs. Margaret, a recent Vassar graduate, wears an elegant, slightly daring wedding gown, knee-length and without sleeves, set off by an elaborate lace headband that covers her forehead like a flapper's; attached to the headband, a copious train of tulle and lace swirls in front of her. She looks shyly pleased. Ben, in a swallowtail morning coat and wing collar, stares straight into the camera with a look that can be construed as resigned or bemused. It's less than two weeks since Wise had ordained him as a member of his first graduating class at the Jewish Institute of Religion, a seminary the great man had founded

to produce socially active and outspoken rabbis, more or less in his own image. Having taken the young Californian who's not yet twenty-four into the rabbinate, Rabbi Wise now has taken him into his family. His son, James Waterman Wise, is the best man.

The new rabbi, not all that far removed from the failing grape farm outside Sacramento where he'd plowed behind a mule, might have been excused if he thought he now had a special relationship with his rabbinic elder. He had room for a father figure. His own father had died when he was fifteen; before that, as Ben remembered him, he had been a convalescent porch-sitter leaving the active work to the children and his strong-willed, much younger wife. But Ben has not become an intimate and protégé of Stephen Wise, for the simple reason that Wise does not cultivate intimates and protégés; he has followers. His closest clerical friend, the liberal Unitarian John Haynes Holmes, described Wise as a man who was never quite comfortable

speaking to small groups. "He had a keen sense of humor, a conta-
gious gaiety of spirit, great charm of personality but a certain unfitness in a room many sizes too small for him," Holmes wrote.
"But let the gathering leap to a thousand people, and the speaker is
in his element . . . Twenty thousand and the speaker has found himself. He moves now with ease and immeasurable passion."

That "certain unfitness" could be an explanation for the look
on Ben's face that the photographer happened to catch. For all his
humor, spirit, and charm, the great man may have left Ben feeling
that this intimate family wedding was a public event, little different

for him from hundreds he'd performed. There is a further layer of complexity here that would give Ben and Margaret a context for interpreting their Alabama experience a few years later. One of her grandfathers had served as president of Temple Emanu-El, the cathedral of well-to-do Jews of German origin who carried themselves as a separate social aristocracy in New York, with their own clubs, balls, and hospitals mirroring the institutions of the dominant gentile elite. Her mother, who regularly toured the Continent, summered in the Adirondacks, and referred to the future president of the United States as "Franklin" even though she had never met him, belonged to that well-defined class. But, as everyone knew, the turning point in Stephen Wise's career had been his very public rejection at age thirty-two of an offer to become Temple Emanu-El's rabbi, on grounds that it would not allow its spiritual leader to espouse views contrary to the views and interests of the temple's trustees. Stephen Wise would not be a captive of that class, its pet priest. So he established a congregation of his own called the Free Synagogue, where his freedom to speak his mind would be a founding principle, secured forever. That's what was "Free" about it.

His opening of a new seminary was a further challenge to the Jewish establishment. Unlike Hebrew Union College in Cincinnati, it would be Zionist and specifically concerned with social outreach to the poor and persecuted, non-Jews as well as Jews. The counsel Stephen Wise offered Ben's class, the first rabbis trained in his shadow, was in no way avuncular. It was from Ezekiel and strenuously prophetic: *Son of man, stand upon thy feet; and I shall speak with thee; and men, whether they hear or whether they forbear, shall know that I, the Lord, thy God, have sent thee.* And so it came to pass that Ben Goldstein, whose thesis as a student rabbi happens to have been on Ezekiel, went forth in this spirit.

HEARTIEST CONGRATULATIONS UPON CALL   DEEPLY REJOICE IN YOUR
NEW OPPORTUNITY   AFFECTIONATE GREETINGS   Stephen Wise's Western Union telegram reached Ben Goldstein in Berkeley in January
1929. Fresh out of the seminary, Ben had moved with his bride to
Champaign, Illinois, to take a post at the university there in the
original chapter of the nascent Hillel movement that my dad was
one day to lead. Then he had shifted to the University of California,
his alma mater, also for Hillel. Finally, thanks to shrewd brokering
by Wise himself when he'd become aware four months earlier that
the rabbi of Temple Beth Or in Montgomery might be moving, Ben
had gotten his "call" to Alabama. Another sponsor was my pal Bobby
Schoenfeld's future rabbi, Louis Newman, a Wise disciple Ben had
known in New York who was then holding forth in San Francisco.
Wise assured his stepniece that Montgomery was "a lovely little town"
where Ben would gain "something he has never had—charge of a
community." The question of whether the pulpit would be "free"
didn't arise.

The town was Jefferson Davis's capital, the seat of the Confed-
eracy, when Montgomery's Jewish congregation dedicated its first
synagogue in 1862. Its constitution had been written in German ten
years earlier by its original elders, merchants mostly. Some of their
sons were serving in the Confederate forces. That first house of prayer,
a sweet little Romanesque building where the men originally did the
worshipping while the women sat apart in the balcony, still stands
at the corner of Church and Catoma. It has been a Church of Christ
since 1905, after the Jewish congregation moved to a larger, more
imposing domed sanctuary nearby, the one Ben Goldstein inherited,
on Clayton and Sayre. It had taken only a generation for Montgomery's Jews to abandon the traditional ritual. Starting in 1874,
women were allowed to worship with men, men were allowed to
pray with their heads uncovered, and, self-consciously following the
practice of Temple Emanu-El in New York, Beth Or switched to a

service more in English than Hebrew. The Reform path had been blazed by an up-and-coming cotton broker, Emanuel Lehman, who had served on the committee that drafted the Montgomery congregation's German constitution. This founding father then moved his family brokerage firm, Lehman Brothers, to New York, where it branched out from cotton to such new commodities as petroleum, coffee, and sugar. Emanuel and his brother Mayer, who followed him out of Montgomery, regularly worshipped at Emanu-El with Margaret Goldstein's grandfather.

That was almost a connection, but Margaret, who had no talent for ingratiating herself, didn't exploit it. She's remembered still, by the handful of Montgomery Jews who are old enough to remember her at all, as a condescending northerner with a habit of tossing off remarks for their shock value. Ben, who arrived in Montgomery several weeks before Herbert Hoover's inauguration and left a couple of months after Franklin Roosevelt's, is remembered as dynamic, intellectual, and "controversial." Neither of the two histories of the congregation that have since been written mentions that he was all but run out of town on a rail. (They also don't mention that one of his predecessors, a Rabbi Messing, had to leave within twenty-four hours in 1908 when he was caught, so oral tradition has it, living up to his name with the wife of a prominent gentile.)

Ben would later write that he'd been warned from the very start by leaders of his congregations not to speak about "the Negro question." It was not something an outsider could readily understand, went the argument, nor was it an issue on which Jews, who had their own problems, wanted to set themselves apart. So in his first couple of years in Alabama he spoke boldly but elliptically, walking to the very edge of what could be said and now and then sticking his toe just over the line, allowing himself to be provocative without frontally assaulting the South's racial code. Asked to address the Women's Club of Montgomery in November 1929, when he had been in town only eight months, he chose "Citizenship in the Broadest Sense" as his theme and declared that "the right to vote should be given to all citizens." He didn't explicitly say that black Alabamans were citizens, however, so whatever slight shiver went through the audience of upper-crust southern white women soon passed. "Practice must conform to our ideals," the young rabbi went on, "and when practice fails to measure up to our ideals, we must condemn the practice." Daring but not suicidal, he did not yet find it in himself to condemn any particular local customs.

That kind of talk gained him some adherents, southern Jews who wanted to feel that they too were not illiberal, that they too were in touch with advanced thought. Ben conducted ambitious study groups, including one on philosophy that drew venturesome Christians as well as members of the congregation, and started a lecture series that brought thinkers such as Bertrand Russell to Montgomery. Summing up his activities early on in a letter to Stephen Wise, he sounds lighthearted: "I have spoken (with authoritative gesture and manners) on 'the woman in business,' 'the future of America' (declaring it has none), 'what we can think of God' . . . [and] 'how to rear children' . . . I feel like a magazine."

He was also active in support of a new art museum and initiated an annual drive for local and national charities. As the Depression deepened, his sermons and study groups dwelled increasingly on issues of economic and social justice. Judaism was not a religion, he told his students and congregants, but a culture or civilization that passed on a set of ethical imperatives worthy of study. It had no dogmas on God or an afterlife, both of which, according to the rabbi, were optional, indeed dubious, concepts as commonly understood. Ben's adherents, mostly women and young people, found this kind of thinking exciting. It was hardly what they were used to hearing. Many of the men who held the purse strings of the congregation weren't so sure. A handful were soon up in arms, especially after he started harping on the miserable wages paid locally to work-

ers and servants. The arguments he made from the pulpit he'd continue with even less caution at parties. Those who weren't drawn to
him considered him a scold, someone to be admired perhaps, but
shunned. Attendance at Friday night services began to fall off.

Leo Drum, one of the octogenarians I met in Montgomery, was
a student in Ben's confirmation class in 1929 at the age of fourteen
and then in a post-confirmation class that studied the New Testament to prepare young Jews, the rabbi said, to get on in a society
that pretended to live by its precepts. He remembered his father remarking to the rabbi that he was sorry that attendance at Friday services was so poor. "I'd just as soon speak to empty benches as empty
heads," Ben replied, so Leo Drum's father told his son. The thought
that Ben might be feeling frustrated does not seem to have occurred
to the elder Drum. He thought his rabbi simply arrogant and he
wasn't alone. *Whether they hear or whether they forbear*, the prophet
had said. In Ben's Montgomery congregation, some were hearing,
many forbearing.

All that was *before* he finally crossed the line and got himself
branded in the wider community as someone who adhered to the
subversive doctrine of "social equality" between black and white.
As Ben was starting his third year in Montgomery, the Scottsboro
case began its long, clamorous, twisting and twisted history, becoming a thirties version of what the Sacco and Vanzetti case had
been for the twenties: an international cause, a moral touchstone,
an organizing opportunity, a political stepping-stone. It would take
eleven trials—all but one ending in swift verdicts of guilty by all-
white juries—two landmark appeals to the United States Supreme
Court, and more than nineteen years before the legal and political
storm that swirled up on March 25, 1931, with the arrest on rape
charges of nine black "boys," ranging in age from twelve to twenty,
finally exhausted itself with the release of the last of the nine from
an Alabama jail. Thus the case still hadn't ended when I met Ben
Lowell in the summer of 1948: Heywood Patterson, a Scottsboro ac-

cused who'd been sentenced to death three times and to seventy-five years at his fourth trial, was the object of a manhunt, having just escaped from a prison work gang; Andrew Wright, the last Scottsboro "boy" left in jail, was nearly two years away from parole.

The crux of the case was whether the word of nine illiterate blacks could be taken over that of two white women. In the Alabama of 1931, this was not really a question. Virginia Price and Ruby Bates claimed to have been ravished by each of these young blacks in turn on an open car of a freight train traveling slowly in broad daylight across northern Alabama on its way from Chattanooga to Memphis. Here was the archetypal crime. The whole racial order turned on an idea amounting to a mystique: that the purity of white womanhood was everywhere menaced by black depravity. It didn't matter that the supposed victims in this case were tramps in the two most obvious senses of the word, that they bore no signs of physical assault when medically examined an hour and a half after the supposed attacks, that they were cool and composed as rape victims seldom are, or that the only traces of sperm cells in their vaginas were no longer moving on their own, meaning the semen could only have been deposited before they boarded the train. It didn't even create a reasonable doubt when Ruby Bates eventually changed her story and testified for the defense that they'd never been touched. For those slight flaws in the prosecution only became conspicuous after the first four trials had been completed in whirlwind fashion at the Jackson County courthouse in Scottsboro within two weeks of the arrests, resulting in eight death sentences and one mistrial. (Heeding the prosecutor, two members of the final jury held out against sending the twelve-year-old, Roy Wright, to the electric chair; the other ten found no reason to spare him.) White Alabama congratulated itself on not having lynched the obvious culprits, an outcome prevented by an anti-Klan governor who dispatched the National Guard to Scottsboro. It was outraged when outsiders, overlooking this achievement, asked how white juries could possibly reach a fair verdict with an angry white mob, sometimes numbering several thousand, waiting outside on the courthouse square; or pointed out that the defense lawyers had never even met their clients before the start of the trials and so weren't aware that prosecutors had hinted to some of them that they might be spared if they shifted the guilt onto the others. Once the Communist Party, operating through a front called the ILD for International Labor Defense, wrested control of the defense from the NAACP, white Alabama knew why it was being subjected to such nitpicking. It was Communists and only Communists who were keeping the case—and the defendants—alive.

Though that's what Ben Goldstein would eventually conclude—fatefully, for himself at least—he didn't instantly leap into the case, which was soon the subject of Communist-engineered demonstrations in places as far afield as Harlem, Dresden, and Moscow. That summer, he and Margaret were away in Europe on a long trip paid for by her mother. So it wasn't until September that he uttered the word "Scottsboro" in a sermon. He waited for Yom Kippur, the day of atonement; the trials, he said, were an example of the harm prejudice can do. By then the Scottsboro boys had been jailed in Montgomery for five months on Kilby Prison's death row, but Ben hadn't been to see them. By the next Yom Kippur, in 1932, he had visited them several times. Death row turned out to be a corridor with a dozen cells ending in the room with the electric chair. It left an impression. So this Yom Kippur Ben allowed himself to dwell a little longer on the case. Hasty verdicts take years to remedy, he said, asking his congregation to think about "the horror of keeping youth in that kind of confinement for two years." No other white clergyman in Alabama had gone to Kilby to see the Scottsboro accused or spoken out in such terms.

There were protests at Beth Or, not for the first time. Earlier that year, a letter in the temple's archive reveals, the school committee had been asked to investigate a sensational charge that Marxism was being inculcated in the Sunday school. "The rumor that Communistic thoughts are being given to the children particularly in the post-confirmation class is without foundation," its chairman reported back. When a vote was taken on Ben's reelection at a congregational meeting in April 1932, forty-one persons had voted for renewing his contract; only nine had been ready to be counted against him. The congregation even bought him a new Chrysler to replace his old Essex. But by January 1933 the president of the congregation, a devoted Goldstein supporter named Simon Wampold who had earlier praised the rabbi's "fearless expression of beliefs and honest convictions," was writing in desperation to Stephen Wise, imploring the great man to "convince Ben it is to his personal interest to soft pedal his interest in the Negro problem."

No answer has been preserved. It's hardly likely that Wise, who had launched Ben with the injunction to "stand upon thy feet," would tell him to take it easy. At most, he might have passed a message through his sister-in-law to Margaret counseling a little prudence in picking his fights. But that's why Wampold, whose term as president was ending, was writing in the first place. Ben was now picking fights without regard to consequences. At his last board meeting, Wampold had ruled a motion to discuss the rabbi's activities out of order. By then Ben had taken his "interest in the Negro problem" beyond the synagogue and Kilby Prison. As publicly as he could, he had taken it all the way to the end of Dexter Street, to the governor's office in the state capitol, and from there to embattled Tallapoosa County, where white posses had been hunting black sharecroppers after a gunfight over title to several cows and a mule that had been portrayed in the *Montgomery Advertiser* as a "Red" agrarian uprising. ALABAMA DEPUTIES BATTLE ARMED NEGRO COMMUNISTS, a headline on December 20, 1932, screamed.

What must have set tongues wagging all over white Montgomery, from Jews of Ben's congregation to members of the country club that barred them, was the astonishing committee that Ben put together for his call three days later on Governor Benjamin Meeks Miller, the man who had prevented lynchings by sending the National Guard to Scottsboro. There was the rabbi, who would have been regarded as an outsider by virtue of being a Jew even if he'd been born in Montgomery, parading into the capitol with two sisters from the very pinnacle of Montgomery society. Not only were the Craik sisters daughters of one of the founders of the country club, they were direct descendants of George Washington's personal physician, Mount Vernon neighbor, and close friend James Craik, who had bled the first president (possibly to death) during what proved to be his final illness, then closed his eyes. Their father, George William Craik, had been president in his day of the Mobile and Montgomery Railroad and vice president of the First National Bank of Montgomery. Jean Nash Read, the older of the two sisters, presided over a salon at Hazel Hedge, the twenty-acre family estate where she'd entertained the Fitzgeralds. Her sister, Mary Craik Speed, had recently returned with her daughter Jane from a sojourn in Vienna where they had picked up the vocabulary of class struggle.

Months later Mrs. Speed, by then in flaming exile in New York, would write in the *Harlem Liberator* that the citizens' committee had been formed at the urging of a couple of organizers from the Communist Party and International Labor Defense, two lawyers and "several comrades" who had come down from Birmingham. They "wanted action" in the form of a delegation, one the governor would have to receive, that would confront him with a demand for a special investigation of the repression in Tallapoosa. The ILD organizer could have been her daughter Jane Speed, who was soon to become the movement's Alabama representative. Years later this descendant of George Washington's physician would wed a onetime president of Puerto Rico's tiny Communist Party, the novelist César

Andreu Iglesias. The *Harlem Liberator*, the thin weekly in which her mother proudly told her story, was the organ of the League of Struggle for Negro Rights, a Communist front. The *Liberator* offered little plaster busts of the poet Pushkin to its readers the way newspaper circulation departments in those days used to offer cheap dictionaries or encyclopedias to new subscribers, but its press run stayed mired in the hundreds. Neither Pushkin busts nor copies of the paper found their way to Montgomery, so no one there is likely to have noticed when Mrs. Speed boasted to the comrades in Harlem about the mission she and Ben had undertaken, thus confirming as clearly as possible the worst suspicions of Rabbi Goldstein's critics as to his involvement with Communists.

Whether this was Ben's first contact with the party is open to question. If his FBI file is to be believed, party records in Los Angeles later declared that the first of his two separate periods of membership began in 1932: in other words, in Alabama. At about the same time, one of the discussion groups he led was becoming a kind of "way station" for union organizers passing quietly through town, a place for succor and earnest discussion, as Olive Stone, a sociologist at a local college for women, recalled much later in an oral history interview. Ben was usually the contact person for the visitors but he was still thinking for himself. The group's discussions were never doctrinaire. "Rabbi Goldstein loved to talk about teleological questions and a whole range of social philosophy," Stone said.

It was Mrs. Speed, the widow of an Episcopal bishop, and her daughter who imported a party line. Ben may have gotten to know the Craik sisters through their brother-in-law, Dr. Charles Pollard, his neighbor on South Perry Street. However the committee was formed, white Montgomery would have no doubt about who was leading whom astray. It had to be the outsider, the "eternal alien" (to dredge up W. J. Cash's epithet for Jews in *The Mind of the South*).

Governor Miller, a starchy Presbyterian, was cordial till he learned the purpose of the visit. Then he stiffened, finally telling his visitors that if they wanted an investigation they could make it themselves. A statement by the committee appeared in the *Advertiser* on Christmas Day. It spoke of "exploitation" by white landowners, of "unscrupulous and oftentimes unfair bookkeeping which took advantage of the ignorance of the Negro," and of the right of share-croppers to organize. In fact, attempts had been under way for a year to form a sharecroppers' union in Tallapoosa. The clash and manhunts of December were not the first. They had been preceded by a shoot-out in July 1931 after the sheriff and his deputies broke up a union meeting at a small rural church near a place called Camp Hill. The idea that the sharecroppers were rebelling was wildly exag-gerated, but for the first time ever thereabouts, they put up some re-sistance. Blacks had to abandon their shacks and flee deep into the pine-covered hills after both clashes so long as carloads of vengeful rifle-toting whites patrolled the roads as if it were hunting season, which it was. In each case, there were shootings and killings. To this day, no one can say for sure how many. Having seen the governor, Ben visited Cliff James, a wounded Tallapoosa black and the owner of the disputed livestock who had been jailed in Montgomery as a ringleader rather than hospitalized. Then, on Christmas Day or the day after, he drove with Mrs. Speed up to Tallapoosa to do the in-vestigating Miller had challenged them to do. They were probably there only a few hours, but using Cliff James's name, Ben found his way to members of the sharecroppers' union. They also met the sheriff's son, who vowed to "get 'em all" and fulminated about "out-siders." A day or two later, James was allowed to die of his wounds in jail.

The trip of the rabbi and the matron to Tallapoosa during a spasm of racial rage in the hills of the Black Belt took courage, more probably than they themselves recognized when they set out. It showed clearly that, however far he had gone in his politics until then, Ben was now prepared to go much further than anyone might have imagined an Alabama rabbi could go in 1932 or '33 (or, for that matter, 1943, '53, or '63). On his return to Montgomery, he invited black ministers to his home and organized a collection of food and clothing for the families of the sharecroppers who were still being hunted in Tallapoosa County. Then the curtain went up on the second round of Scottsboro trials. The Supreme Court had ordered new trials in a place other than Jackson County's now notorious seat. Early in March the date was set. The second round of trials would start in Decatur, a town not so different from Scottsboro and just fifty miles to the west, on March 27.

Other things were happening in this time span. Hitler had come to power in Germany only weeks before; Franklin Roosevelt had just taken his oath. But in the eyes of those engaged in the court struggle, Decatur became the center of the world for a few weeks, the place where the authority of Alabama courts and Alabama juries of a particular hue would be preserved or shaken.

If the NAACP had succeeded in making Clarence Darrow the chief defense counsel in the Scottsboro case as it had tried to do in 1931, Ben might have been able to hold on in Montgomery a little longer. But his fate was probably sealed the moment Samuel Leibowitz, a flamboyant criminal lawyer from Brooklyn, arrived in Alabama in the middle of March to take charge of the case of the seven defendants who were to be retried in Decatur. Leibowitz attempted to ingratiate himself by saying at the first opportunity that he had no sympathy with Communists, no patience for agitators, no desire to tell Alabama how to run its courts. He was a Democrat, he said, there simply to save "innocent boys." At his side was Joseph Brodsky, the chief counsel of the ILD. White Alabama didn't see a Democrat and a Communist. It didn't see two lawyers. It saw two New York Jews. Alabama Jews knew it was time to hunker down, but the case for caution was lost on Ben.

It wasn't lost on Montgomery's mayor, William Gunter, whose political stance was defined by his opposition to the lawlessness of the Ku Klux Klan. The anti-Klan forces had won the upper hand in Alabama's white politics with the election of Governor Miller, thanks in some measure to the crusading of the editor of the *Montgomery Advertiser*, Grover Cleveland Hall, who had won a Pulitzer Prize for his denunciations of the Klan. It was not a position they were about to squander for the seven wayward black youths going on trial again in Decatur. They would not question the original Scottsboro verdicts, not if that meant conceding that the outsiders who were protesting and agitating might have a point. "Carpetbagger buzzards," "apostles of revolution," "drill sergeants of hatred," and "sinister alien influences," editor Hall called them. In the view of the mayor (the same Gunter who's memorialized to this day at Maxwell-Gunter Air Force Base), an out-of-control rabbi, a conspicuous Hebrew who didn't know his place, would have seemed a crazy gift to the Klan, an invitation to reactivate itself in Montgomery.

The evening before the court was to convene in Decatur, Ben was among nine speakers—six black and three white—scheduled to address a meeting at a Birmingham church where funds were to be raised for the Scottsboro defense. A couple of days before the meeting a local paper carried a headline playing up the local angle. GOLDSTEIN STUMPS FOR SCOTTSBORO 7, it said. That was too much for the board of his temple, which passed a formal resolution appointing a committee "to go to Rabbi Goldstein and ask him to desist from going to Birmingham under all circumstances and desist from doing anything further in the Scottsboro case."

Ben went anyway. If the *Daily Worker* didn't inflate the count, a crowd of a thousand crammed the church while hundreds milled outside. Later Ben agreed to chair another meeting in Birmingham protesting the inevitable guilty verdict in the first of the trials. By then, seeking to quiet the storm, the new president of the congregation

Easter Sunday Has Not Come for the Nine Lads in the
SHADOW OF DEATH

CIVIC MEETING
ON THE
Scottsboro Case

Introduction: A. Johnston, 1st Bapt. Church, Graymont

Chairman: Dr. BENJ. B. GOLDSTEIN
Rabbi, Temple Beth-Or, Montgomery

SPEAKERS
BISHOP B. G. SHAW

DR. HOWARD KESTER
Southern Director, Fellowship of Reconciliation

ADA WRIGHT
Mother of Two of the Scottsboro Boys

BRIEF TALKS BY—

P. D. DAVIS, President, Birmingham Civic Association
BROOKS FULMER, Student, Birmingham-Southern College
MISS JANE SPEED, Member, International Labor Defense
ERNEST SHELL, Student, Miles College; Editor, "The Milean"

White Citizens Are Invited

At 1st Baptist Church, Graymont
Weaver Street & 8th Avenue, West

SUNDAY, APRIL 16, at 3:00 P. M.

Auspices: CITIZENS SCOTTSBORO AID COMMITTEE
of Birmingham, Alabama

had pressed Ben to let him announce that the rabbi would not seek an extension of his contract, which still had five months to run. He wanted it to appear that it had been Ben's own choice. Ben accepted the ultimatum but promptly let it be known that he'd been ousted for outspokenness on racial issues. It was just a few days later that the county prosecutor in Decatur seized the opportunity to exploit the resentment over Leibowitz, Brodsky, and their ilk. Capping a string of nasty anti-Semitic wisecracks in his summing up at the first trial, he pointed to the defense table where the two lawyers sat and demanded that the jury "show them that Alabama justice cannot be bought and sold with Jew money from New York."

Now that the confrontation had been openly framed as Jews vs. Alabama, Temple Beth Or and Mayor Gunter had to decide whether Montgomery could take several months more of a Ben Goldstein who'd been out of control even before he no longer had a job to protect. Just when the mayor started talking with members of the congregation about getting their rabbi out of town is unclear. On May 10 he rammed through a criminal anarchy ordinance making it a crime for two or more persons to gather to study subversive materials. Members of the congregation were told it was aimed at their rabbi and his matronly cohort, Mrs. Speed. Jimmy Loeb, a third-generation cotton merchant, told me his dad was one of a delegation from the congregation that was summoned to see Gunter, who, according to a contemporaneous account passed on to Ben, warned them that Jewish businesses could face a boycott and that the Klan might target their rabbi, even their own homes. He also charged, according to that version, that Ben was an agent of the ILD. That, at least, is what they heard; whether it's also what the mayor actually said or a panicky translation of indirect warnings blandly conveyed, would have been hard to know then, let alone now. What they thought they heard could have been a playback of their own worst fears: if he spoke in general terms of the importance of preserving harmony and order in Montgomery, of keeping the Jewish community from becoming a target, the mayor might not have had to mention burning crosses for Jewish leaders to picture them. Making the warnings more graphic than they had actually been might have been a way for the leaders to say to their rabbi, his supporters, and themselves, "Look, we had no choice."

What's clear is that it took no further pushing for the temple's leaders to tell Ben it was time for him to depart. Ben responded by going to see the mayor, who denied making the remarks that had been attributed to him. On May 14 the board voted him a leave of absence effective immediately, with full pay till the end of his contract. Later the official version became that it had done so at his request and that any difficulties he had with the congregation were over his unorthodox theological views. After Ben told his story on his arrival in New York to a *Times* reporter, the mayor denied that he had ever mentioned a boycott or the Klan. Dutifully, the leaders of the congregation then expressed shock that their departed rabbi could have strayed so far from the truth. MANY JEWS DENY GOLD-STEIN STATEMENT, a banner headline on the front page of the *Alabama Journal* declared.

Ben then wrote a letter to one of the board members, a physician he had valued as a friend, saying the mayor had "the Jews of Montgomery on the run trying to deny something which he created and spread." They all knew the truth, he said, which was that he was told "to get out of Montgomery to save the Jews." He hated "to go like a common convict," he wrote, "but to have you people lie about it later . . . makes me feel worse than ever."

Ben's most relentless antagonist in the congregation, a businessman named Charles Moritz, wrote a surprisingly candid letter to the leading Reform rabbi in Philadelphia explaining why Ben had to go. He had been "preaching and practicing social equality," the letter says, and "consorting with radicals and reds." Moritz, who was to die soon after Ben left town, sounds apoplectic. He calls Ben a "pseudo rabbi," a Communist, and an atheist but still gives him his due. "Goldstein is a brilliant writer and speaker," he says, "but he doesn't fit in our Southern civilization." That phrase, "our Southern civilization," has a pitiable eloquence in this context, revealing as it does a hunger to believe that Temple Beth Or should "fit in" and does fit in, even if its leaders haven't yet achieved the summum bonum of admission to the Montgomery Country Club. It says they'll always stand with those who exclude them, instead of those far more grievously excluded whom they also exclude.

Moritz then draws the parallel to Leibowitz and Brodsky, who, he says, are "prejudicing the whole state against Jews and N.Y. communistic lawyers." The letter doesn't mention the mayor in explaining Ben's Alabama downfall, but as a clincher, it does say: "Some of our best Christian citizens wondered why we tolerated him as long as we did." A little later, just before he died, Moritz tossed a last stone at the back of his departing rabbi. "No less a person," he wrote, "than John Haynes Holmes"—Stephen Wise's liberal sidekick—had declared Ben Goldstein "unworthy of being in the rabbinate." A publication called the *Montgomery Weekly* said Ben had "gone back north, where he really belonged all the time." Actually, he was a westerner who had come to Montgomery from California, but as a carpetbagger, meddler, and Jew, he defined himself as northern in Alabama minds. And, in fact, he and Margaret landed in Manhattan.

They arrived toward the end of May 1933 in a swirl of emotions, compounded from the Scottsboro cause, Ben's acute sense of injury, and the inconsistent charges and tributes that trailed him all the way from Montgomery. In a few weeks he was introduced to a twenty-year-old ex-editor of a college newspaper who said he was on his way to Cincinnati to study to become a rabbi. When Ben and my dad next met fifteen years later they had identical recollections of Ben's response.

"Don't!" he said.

But he didn't immediately shut down his own life as a rabbi. He wanted vindication. Stephen Wise had the Goldsteins over for an evening and heard them out, listening with carefully measured sympathy to their indignant rendering of what happened between them and Ben's Montgomery congregation and how finally, inevitably, he was pushed out. Wise even invited his former student to be the speaker at the commencement luncheon at the Jewish Institute of Religion, his rabbinic alma mater. And later he passed on Holmes's response to the canard that he had read Ben out of the liberal clergy. His friend denied ever having said any such thing, "as if Holmes would stoop to speak ill of anyone," Wise then wrote to Margaret's mother, "least of all someone for whom he cares as genuinely as he does for Ben."

Beyond that, Stephen Wise was conspicuously absent from the debate over Ben's ouster, which swiftly made its way onto the agenda of the CCAR, the Central Conference of American Rabbis, Reform Judaism's clerical guild where the renowned New Yorker was regarded with a wary awe, tinged by jealousy. Perhaps he thought the family connection made it inappropriate for him to jump in. Perhaps, for once, he was sensitive to rabbinic politics: the president of the CCAR that year happened to be Alabama's most prominent rabbi, Morris Newfield, who had managed to steer clear of racial controversy in nearly four decades in Birmingham. Newfield had rushed down to Montgomery to make an investigation of the circumstances surrounding Ben's ouster on behalf of his organization but carefully avoided meeting the remnant of Goldstein supporters there. Instead, he was satisfied to play back what had become the congregation's line: that Ben's freethinking on matters theological was the basic cause of his undoing and that his outspokenness on Scottsboro and Tallapoosa was never more than an irritant. In more than one sense, the Alabama rabbi's report was a whitewash. But it meant that for the CCAR to take a stand now in favor of Ben, it would have to repudiate its own president and, by extension, all southern Jews who wanted nothing to do with racial controversy, which meant the vast majority. Still, taking a stand in defense of Ben's lost cause in Montgomery was what the chairman of its Social Justice Committee, a Baltimore rabbi named Edward Israel, felt it had to do. Israel believed the CCAR needed to defend the freedom of all rabbis to speak out on pressing moral and social concerns.

This was the principle that had defined Stephen Wise's career. Wise happened to be a member of Israel's committee as well as of the executive committee of the CCAR. But though he corresponded with both Newfield and Israel in 1933, he never once mentioned Ben. Yes, he might have felt the constraint of family. Yes, he might have tried to avoid upsetting Rabbi Newfield. But hesitation on either ground would not have been characteristic. The real reason for his unaccustomed reticence cannot be documented but seems obvious. Given Ben's alignment with the International Labor Defense over Scottsboro, there was every suspicion that he had gotten too close to Communists. Wise, as might be expected of this man of many causes, was willing to write letters on behalf of the Scottsboro accused; but along with other supporters of the NAACP, he kept his distance from the Communist-controlled ILD, which had charge of the Scottsboro defense. He didn't sign petitions its sympathizers circulated and had his secretary send a dismissive reply when, three months before Ben reached New York, the Scottsboro New Trial Emergency Fund wrote under an ILD letterhead asking Wise to use his influence with Jewish periodicals to get them to support its appeal. He was "definitely persuaded," the reply said, that the fund could manage without him.

Ben had clearly crossed a line as far as Wise was concerned. He would give him dinner and a hearing for the sake of Margaret and his sister-in-law, but he wouldn't back him in the CCAR and wouldn't find him a new congregation. Writing to Wise years later, Ben would refer to an "occasion on which you told me I could never be a Rabbi again, or engage in Jewish work," an encounter that seems likeliest to have come in Ben's first months back in New York. What it amounted to for Ben was rejection by the rabbi on whom he thought he had modeled himself, for Wise's approval mattered more to Ben than his string-pulling. For Ben it was a choice, finally, of allegiances, and if he didn't know it already, he now found that he had pledged his. "I sometimes think I learned some of the things you said too well," he would write six and a half years later when he'd gotten over the reverence in which he'd held his wife's stepuncle, although maybe not his own self-righteousness.

If any of Ben's rabbinic peers ever commended him for his brave stand in Alabama, it was in private. A special committee was appointed at the CCAR's annual meeting in 1933 to report back on the Goldstein matter the following year. In 1934 its report still wasn't ready. By 1935 Ben Goldstein had slipped off the agenda. "My personal feeling," Rabbi Israel wrote Newfield's successor as president, "is that we hardly faced this case with the same forthright courage that we face the troubles in the other fellow's back yard," In any case, whether Ben thought he had abandoned the rabbinate or that the rabbinate had abandoned him, by 1935 he was effectively out.

I'm half amused to feel my excitement as I lay out my little trove of ancient CCAR documents. It's as if the senior citizen I've now become is on the verge of cracking some big story. All of these minutes, statements, and letters were drafted before I was born, before my dad was a rabbi, decades before he had his own ceremonial turn as president of the CCAR. None of what I'm discovering matters now to anyone in the world except me and Jo Rogers, Ben's daughter down in Knoxville, plus a couple of Goldstein nieces in Cali-

fornia. But I sense I'm getting as close as I'll ever get to the core of a mystery that has fascinated me for more than half a century, the question of what drove Ben down his winding path to the point where I finally met him. Was it the Scottsboro outrage, or a sense of his own righteousness in the face of rejection? Was it injustice or pride? Injustice *and* pride? Did Ben himself know? What's obvious is the result: the fellowship and moral conviction he had looked for in the rabbinate he now sought elsewhere.

On his own, he drifted with the current of the left, using the title "rabbi" only when it served the cause of the moment or he could pick up a modest honorarium by performing a wedding. He had come North a few days too late to join in an ILD march on the White House on behalf of the Scottsboro accused. Otherwise he might have accompanied Ruby Bates, the reformed rape victim who had just recanted her earlier testimony on the stand in Decatur, when she went inside to meet an aide to President Roosevelt. ("This working class girl has the innate fighting spirit of the working class," the *Daily Worker* said.) But Rabbi Benjamin Goldstein soon showed up with Mrs. Speed on the national council of the League of Struggle for Negro Rights, the Communist front, which had Langston Hughes as its nominal president. That doesn't guarantee that Ben ever met the poet, for the league had its existence almost entirely on paper. It was his last recorded involvement in the Scottsboro case or, indeed, the broader struggle for racial equality. Given that he left Montgomery twenty-one years before the arrival there of a cerebral young preacher named Martin Luther King, Jr., he can be said to have been ahead of his time. But if that's true, he wouldn't even live to see his time.

In New York, where he moved with Margaret into an apartment house called the Yucatan opposite the City College campus on Amsterdam Avenue, Ben's new political horizon soon became international. As Rabbi Goldstein, he appeared in Chicago in September 1934 for a "congress" of one of the more successful front groups of the thirties, the American League Against War and Fascism, which drew more than three thousand delegates to its meeting. Most of the delegates were not Communists, but the party controlled the congress. Earl Browder, the party leader, was elected to the resolutions committee, a mixed bag that contained Communists, civil libertarians, clergymen, and Ben, who had ties to each of these groups. A few years later Rabbi Goldstein reemerged from obscurity to chair meetings for still another front at the onset of the civil war in Spain, the American Committee to Aid Spanish Democracy. Meanwhile, working a connection traceable to Scottsboro, Ben was getting into movie distribution under the nom de guerre George Stern.

At first, his business was agitprop. His connection was Tom Brandon, a former truck driver who had aspirations to make documentary films that could be used to mobilize the masses the way early Soviet filmmakers had tried to do in the twenties in the service of the vanguard party. Brandon had traveled south to make a documentary on the Scottsboro case with two similarly motivated comrades, a 35 mm Bell & Howell Eyemo movie camera, and a letter on *New York Times* stationery signed by John Martin, which they hoped to pass off as press credentials to Alabama sheriffs who would be unlikely to know that Martin was the paper's dance critic. It seems they never got to test the letter's efficacy. The New York license plates on their Model T drew a hostile crowd not long after they parked in the courthouse square in Decatur. Or was it Scottsboro? Brandon's memory was obviously shaky by the time he sat down late in life to write his unpublished memoir, which says the trip was in 1931 but describes events that occurred two years later. Whenever it was, not much film was exposed. The three young men based themselves in Tennessee, got new plates, and then ran errands into Alabama and Georgia for Communist organizers for a few months. "The daring and dedicated work of the Communists I met and worked with," Brandon wrote, "struck me, in that atmosphere of hardship, tension and terror, as being remarkable."

Brandon's southern adventure furnished a model for the Workers Film and Photo League, a party offshoot that sent young cameramen out to get footage of demonstrations, strikes, and police repression that could then be shown to party, union, and front meetings as "Workers' Newsreels." The league became significant as a training ground for documentary filmmakers. It also got listed as a subversive organization. Brandon himself soon moved on, getting into distribution on a commercial basis. He founded an outfit called the Brandon Film Corporation that started importing Soviet and other foreign films. By the sixties, having gone from being a young radical to a tightfisted, exploitative entrepreneur, he had cornered the market on the American distribution of the works of Fellini, Antonioni,

Renoir, Resnais, and other great European filmmakers. It's not clear whether Ben met Tom Brandon in the South or through one of the organizers Brandon had met on his trip, but Ben's doppelgänger George Stern became an early employee of Brandon's company. By 1936 Stern was listed as vice president of Garrison Films, a Brandon offshoot specializing in Soviet films. It was Brandon who apparently suggested that Ben use an alias. It wasn't because there was anything clandestine about the work. Probably it was just rabbi avoidance, a way of sorting out Ben's phone calls. It couldn't be good for the business to have ideologically motivated customers in Pittsburgh, Youngstown, or Milwaukee wondering why they'd been put through to a clergyman when they called to lease a print of *Battleship Potemkin*.

When Ben moved with his family to Los Angeles in 1937, a new division of labor between Goldstein and his double Stern surfaced. Goldstein went as the West Coast representative of a Soviet film company sometimes called Artinko, sometimes Amkino, a division of Amtorg, a Soviet trading company that provided cover for spies as a matter of routine. Both Goldstein and Stern had to look for jobs since Artinko didn't pay much beyond commissions that were less than a sure thing, for when party branches and front groups wanted films, they often had to be given gratis. Occasionally Hollywood studios would need a little Russian footage for a war film or something historic. *Mission to Moscow* and *Song of Russia*, studio films made in the faint glow of the wartime alliance, may have made 1943 a bonanza year, but if so, it was the only one. At first Goldstein and Stern seemed to go for any kind of white-collar job, including a business venture as part owner of a woolens plant that failed. That was Goldstein's. Later Stern concentrated on Hollywood, where he worked briefly for the Academy of Motion Picture Arts and Sciences as a publicist the year Hitchcock's *Rebecca* won the award for best picture, then for the Technicolor Corporation as a quality-control technician screening master prints in order to detect flaws. The academy dismissed him, it appears, because he was suspected of being a Red. Finally he worked for a small independent outfit called United Films. He may also have done some freelancing for Disney as a technician or publicist. He had social contacts with Hollywood figures later blacklisted for refusing to name names before the House Un-American Activities Committee. Jo Rogers, the former Josie Goldstein, remembers the actor Howard Da Silva visiting their home on more than one occasion, and the FBI later reported Ben's presence at a party at the home of the screenwriter Dalton Trumbo. Except for an occasional wedding performed in his living room, the rabbi wasn't much in evidence.

Hollywood lives don't get much more obscure than this. After he came back East, Ben seemed a vaguely romantic, vaguely chic figure because of his time in California. Artinko and Amkino didn't come up in the stories he told. If he'd ever mentioned them, the illusion we cherished of him as a Hollywood insider trailing clouds of glamour might have popped like a bubble. What exactly this energetic and articulate former rabbi thought he was doing there, why he went and why he stayed for eleven years, are questions that find no particular fit with the available facts. There are two places to turn for answers. One is a long, passionate typed letter he pounded out on New Year's Day, 1940, in response to the first word he'd had from Stephen Wise in several years. The other is the farrago of leads, investigative dead ends, and gossip that the FBI started to accumulate a little more than a year later after its Los Angeles office received a tip in the form of an unsigned four-paragraph letter that began: "I believe it would be well for your Bureau to investigate the activities of a Ben Goldstein who resides at 209 South Wilton Place . . . The writer believes he may be endeavoring to cause trouble in our defense industries. So far as I know, he is not employed, is well dressed, and lives well."

The occasion for Stephen Wise's letter was the Nazi-Soviet pact of September 23, 1939, or, as he called it, "the high, holy peace of the Nazi and Communist saints." It can't have been good for Ben's business in Soviet films, Wise imagines. "I would like to hear from you. I wonder whether it will be possible to go on with your particular work." Wise's light touch is none too light. He sounds like an uncle who can't resist pointing out to an adolescent recovering from a pileup that his advice about booze and fast cars had been worth heeding. But affection also comes through. "I hear the baby is a real roughneck like her Father, not a gentle lady like her Mother," he writes. (The older man may have learned to separate ideology and love. In a letter to John Haynes Holmes he'd complained of the "empoisoning indoctrination" his own fellow-traveling daughter received on a trip to Russia.) Implicitly Wise is showing the way back, offering help, if Ben will only acknowledge that he has strayed, as, Wise seems sure, he must finally have deduced from Stalin's accord with Hitler.

Nearly eighteen years after he entered the great man's seminary, it's still "Dear Dr. Wise" when Ben types his reply on New Year's Day. He's not the only one who couldn't bring himself to write "Dear Stephen." In the Wise archive, there aren't many who took that liberty. Just as Wise couldn't hide his satisfaction at having been right all along about the Communists, Ben cannot conceal his bitterness over the rejection he'd experienced. He observes the norms of courtesy but sarcasm seeps through. "I was considerably surprised at hearing from you directly after all these months and years of silence," he begins, writing on his Amkino Corporation stationery, "and even more surprised to learn that you had been thinking of us at all. We are very appreciative of your thoughtfulness."

What follows is a sort of sermon—three single-spaced pages on the state of the world—the theme of which is that the cowardice, greed, and hypocrisy of the capitalist nations before the Nazis left the Soviet Union with no choice but to accept an accommodation in order to protect its people. What Moscow had done "in the case of Germany and even in the case of Poland and Finland," the onetime rabbi tells his former mentor, was done "for the great mass of the people whom we have professed to love." The Soviet Union is not "on the side of the despisers of mankind." And so on in that vein: earnest, righteous, occasionally eloquent twaddle. Reading it now, I want to say, "Oh, Ben." I can only be grateful the archives haven't yielded my old friend's rationalization for the Moscow trials.

But then, despite myself, I find I'm a little touched by a postscript: "I am at present selling shoes to poor Mexican and Negro children who haven't the money to buy stockings. It is a nice way to find out about the world." Perhaps Stephen Wise, who might well have been offended, was touched too. For Ben's sake, or more likely his sister-in-law's and Margaret's, he turns the other cheek—not one of the Ten Commandments—and writes back as if nothing has changed over the past decade: he has found a pulpit that Ben could occupy comfortably after an absence from the rabbinate of seven years. It's in nearby Santa Monica of all places. He would do his best to make it happen if Ben would only indicate an interest in the position. In fact, he sends along a letter of recommendation. All Ben has to do is put it in the mail. Wise's letter places a tolerant gloss on Ben's politics. "Like many of the young people, he moved towards the Left when the Left gave promise of such a united front as all of us liberals could join in," Wise wrote. "I would love to see him in a place where he could regain his one-time relationship to Jewry and its organized congregational life."

That was too much of a climb down for Ben, who appears never to have posted the letter or replied to Wise. But if he didn't want to go back to being a rabbi, what did he want? Did selling shoes to poor kids without stockings or, later, promoting the Academy Awards provide a sense of purpose? Or was the FBI's anonymous tipster onto something? His most concrete and tantalizing allegation was that Ben was a "personal friend" of a convicted Soviet espionage agent named Mikhail Gorin. The bureau is plodding and easily distracted, constantly masticating the information it collects without ever digesting it. But eventually it establishes that Gorin, whom it believes to be an agent of the NKVD, the Soviet secret police, had been entertained in Goldstein's home. It may even have been that the connection between Ben and Gorin went back to New York, for when Ben was taken on as a distributor of Soviet films, Gorin was using the trading company Amtorg there as his cover. Like Ben, he then moved to California. And he was by no means Ben's only Russian visitor with ties to the NKVD. Boris Morros and Vasily Zubilin were to become more notorious.

Morros was a Russian-born Hollywood producer with family still in the old country. He was already a middling producer at Paramount in the thirties, working on films for Fred Astaire and Laurel and Hardy, when an NKVD recruiter talked him into providing cover for espionage by trading on the well-being of his relatives. Morros's original handler was Zubilin, who then got cover himself in what purported to be a Paramount office in Berlin. A rising figure in the netherworld of Soviet espionage, Zubilin was chosen for a succession of critical assignments: in Poland at the time of the Katyn massacre where he interviewed doomed Polish officers, sparing some who could be used to serve the Kremlin's interests; and then in China. By 1942 he had become the NKVD station chief in the United States. Under his real name, Vasily Zarubin, he would later become a major general, the deputy chief of foreign intelligence for the KGB in Moscow, and a two-time winner of the Order of Lenin. At a party at Ben's house in Los Angeles, so an informer told the FBI, this same Vasily Zubilin or Zarubin played the piano and sang a few songs. That would have been early 1943, when Zubilin visited the West Coast to oversee a network that later penetrated the Manhattan Project.

Could the spymaster, whose importance was not yet recognized by the FBI, have been making an innocent social call on the rabbi? That's one explanation, but maybe not the likeliest. As the agent for Soviet films, Ben had a lot to do with officials of the Russian consulate in Los Angeles. Not only did he entertain them, he went house-hunting for them, helped them settle on a location for their new office, chauffeured them, lent them the family Packard, put visitors up at his house, from which a number of calls were made to people who worked at defense installations in Southern California including both Douglas Aircraft and North American Aviation. The Feds suspected that something was going on, something in the nature of espionage, but nothing ever jelled; they never figured out what Ben was doing if he wasn't just a naïve, infatuated Russophile, a Commie groupie.

He behaves suspiciously—registering under his own name at a hotel in Reno, he unaccountably gives the St. George Hotel in Brooklyn as his home address—but not the way you would expect a secret agent to behave. Entertaining foreign spies in your own living room would seem to be a way to attract attention, not avoid it. If it were just the FBI file, I'd be tempted to write off the record of suspicious comings and goings as so much hearsay and speculation. Besides, although they describe events that occurred a lifetime ago, pages of the file are obliterated in part by blobs of black India ink in order to mask the identity of sources, now long dead, or the bureau's methods in compiling lists of toll calls made on Ben's phone. If the sources still can't be known, how can they be trusted? In fact, however, Jo Rogers distinctly remembers the visits of the Russians. "They were constant guests in our house," she told me. She especially recalls one, perhaps Zubilin, over whom a fuss was made and who made a fuss over her, presenting her with the fanciest dress she'd ever been given. It had puff sleeves and a slightly scooped neck and a long skirt of moiré silk in a fairly bright coral color. Josie, as she then was, wore it downstairs that night at the age of seven or eight and never again, for she had outgrown it by the time she had another special occasion for which it might have been right.

In December 1943, the name Ben Goldstein turns up in two messages to KGB headquarters in Moscow that were eventually decoded by the Signals Security Agency, a forerunner of what's now the National Security Agency, as part of a highly secret decryption project. The project was called Venona, itself a code name that was seldom uttered outside the inner sanctums of spookdom until the 1990s, when finally it was revealed to have been the Rosetta stone of Soviet espionage in America. Venona—so secret that President Truman was apparently never told of its existence—showed that Alger Hiss and others once thought by stubbornly naïve liberals to have been victims of mass hysteria had indeed been spies. Hiss's cryptonym or code name was ALES. Zubilin's was MAXIM. Boris Morros's was FROST. Ben doesn't appear to have had a cryptonym, which means that his name didn't often come up in the traffic to Moscow. The Venona messages also don't describe him as a "probationer," the code word for agent, an omission that's either exculpatory or leaves his status open to question. Nevertheless, the messages seem to nail Ben, too: not for espionage but philandering, a sphere of endeavor in which he had not otherwise been conspicuous. The Soviet consulate in San Francisco, including the KGB station, is in an uproar over his affair with the wife of an official named Mikhail Kalatozov whose cover involves Soviet films. The KGB cables, stamped "Top Secret" and buried in the archives of the NSA for half a century, report the "scandal" of Mrs. Kalatozov's "intimate relations with Ben." Moscow is told that Elena Gorbunoova, a member of the consulate's staff, "personally saw Ben" doing something with Kalatozov's wife. Four words that spelled out what they were doing were not recovered by the cryptographers. They could have been studying a Russian language manual or the Book of Ezekiel, but the context strongly suggests that they were caught in bed. Footnotes to the translations identify all the Russians. The security agency, however, can't pin down Ben Goldstein; he's described as "not known."

Maybe the Kalatozov's affair has something to do with the end of Ben's marriage to Margaret a couple of months later. Maybe it has something to do with an intriguing point on which the memory of Jo Rogers and the FBI file appear to coincide. As if to confirm what her aunt Elsie once said about her parents' divorce, the file reports a conversation about a month after Ben moved out of the house on South Wilton Place in which he is supposed to have said "he expected to be going to Moscow in about three months." The name of the Russian on whom he's counting to smooth his arrival there is blacked out in accord with some arcane FBI regulation. Still, his intention now seems clear. Was Ben coming in from the cold or was war-devastated Stalinist Russia his idea of a promised land? The FBI doesn't speculate about motives, and anyway, after the Kalatozov affair, Moscow was no longer interested in having him, if it ever was. So five years later he was going to ballgames with me in the Bronx, not living in Moscow, when Stalin set a wave of anti-Semitic purges in motion at the time of the phony Doctors' Plot.

Ben's contacts with the Russians appear to dwindle in his last few years in Hollywood. He then allows himself to be more openly involved in Communist Party activities, becoming a member, the FBI's informers report, of Branch S in Hollywood. Later he transfers to the party's Ben Franklin Club in Beverly Hills after he meets the woman who is to become his second wife and moves in with her there on North Alpine Drive, where, instead of a Packard, a 1941 Cadillac is parked in the driveway. My own mother recalled, decades after Ben vanished from our lives, that he said he had been working as a gardener when he met Juliet Lowell. Born Lowenstein and by then a widow with two daughters, she had developed a franchise for herself as a kind of humorist, publishing collections of funny letters laced with double entendres and malapropisms. Juliet and her publisher responded coyly to questions about the authenticity of the letters, so it was never clear whether she was more wit than scavenger or more scavenger than wit. In 1945, the year Ben came into her life and while the war still raged, one of her little books, *Dear Sir*, was second on the *New York Times* bestseller list, a fluffy bit of escapism sandwiched between two different chronicles of the war in Europe from the perspective of the ordinary fighting man, Ernie Pyle's *Brave Men* and Bill Mauldin's *Up Front*. (Juliet's small volume—to give a taste—opens with a letter to a draft board in Los Angeles. "Dear Sir," it says, "I received your notice of Seduction and will be there March 29." It doesn't get much better.)

Four months after the wedding, which was performed by a rabbi, Benjamin Bernard Goldstein became Ben Lowell by order of the Superior Court in Los Angeles. Since he had already had the experience of taking his first wife's name, taking his second's may have seemed the polite thing to do for the sake of his new stepchildren, who, so he was reported to have told a friend, didn't want to be known as Goldsteins. Lowell was "a little too Bostonian," he told a couple of FBI agents who dropped in on him on North Alpine Drive to ask about someone else. But then, he may have reasoned, Juliet's books made her the one who was really invested in a name. Ben's chattiness when the agents came by might have led them to wonder about their ongoing espionage investigation, but once launched, it appears, no amount of rational judgment could bring such an inquiry to a halt.

As if to avoid any chance of confusion, Ben then guaranteed that his new name would get on the blacklist of suspected Communists that the studios would soon compile with the assistance of the House Un-American Activities Committee. In October 1946, he was arrested for illegal picketing in front of Columbia Pictures on behalf of the Conference of Studio Unions, which was at least infiltrated by Communists and which the studios were soon to break. My brother David was briefly married into the family of a CSU veteran who had some footage from that strike on a reel of home movies. When David mentioned Ben to his in-laws, the film was screened for his benefit. Ben, as he now recalls it, was shown sitting on a bench in front of the courthouse where he had to pay a twenty-five-dollar fine. The camera came in for a close-up on a book in his hand. It looked like a prayer book. Ben was smiling. The intent appeared to be mildly satiric or self-mocking, but without a real job, he eventually started casting around for work in his original profession. Now that he was divorced from Margaret, he no longer felt he had a claim on Stephen Wise's attention. But he found a new sponsor, a figure he'd known in his first Hillel job at the University of Illinois twenty years earlier. This was Abram Sachar, a popular historian and lecturer who led the Hillel movement for nearly two decades and had just stepped aside for my dad. Sachar, who was about to launch a new university in Massachusetts named after Justice Louis Brandeis, was spending a season in California when he encountered Ben again. Before recommending Ben for a job, he had one obvious question he felt he needed to ask. Later he was certain he had asked it straight, without euphemism or any ambiguity as to his meaning: Was Ben a Communist?

The seemingly straight answer he got may have been technically accurate, for, according to an FBI informer in the spring of 1948, someone with the initials "B.L." had just been expelled from the Ben Franklin Club for naming names to the Beverly Hills police when they asked for the guest list of a fund-raising party on North Alpine Drive on behalf of *People's World*, the West Coast Communist paper. Once again, Ben's chattiness evidently got the better of him. Either that or he had found an ingenious way to regain rabbinic cover. Legally he had changed his name to Ben Lowell plain and simple, but it was Rabbi Benjamin B. Lowell who now moved back to New York, where I was to meet him at the summer's end on the Hudson River Dayline heading up to Kingston.

So Ben, there you have it—the narrative of your forgotten American life that I had long vowed to piece together if only to satisfy myself. I may not have cracked the story exactly, dispelled its ambiguities or improved on the anticlimax, but that's the way it is with real characters whom we seldom more than glimpse when they're actually crossing our paths. Usually we're too preoccupied with our own static, or the impression we hope to make, to reach beyond the feeble curiosity good manners demand—that slight nod to another's existence that typically comes as an afterthought.

You once did a youngster in early adolescence the favor of drawing him out. I've waited all these years to return it. Now, finally, I feel again that I know you as well as I know most people who are important to me, which is how I felt, after all, at the age of twelve as I sat beside you and Davy in the right-field stands at Yankee Stadium on October 1, 1949, at the next-to-last game of the season; for me still the best baseball game I could ever hope to see. If the Boston Red Sox won the game, they won the pennant. By the third inning, with the Sox already ahead 2–0, the bases loaded, and the whole season at stake, the Yanks had to turn in desperation to their ace reliever Smoky Joe Page, who seldom came into a game before the eighth; never this early. I remember Page striding his long stride in from the bullpen. But then, cruel fate, Smoky Joe couldn't find the strike zone. He started by walking two batters, forcing in two more Boston runs. Doom was written on the scoreboard. 4–0, it said, and the bases were still full with only one out in the third.

Only then did the game become an epic. Our ace pulled himself together, striking out the next two batters, and closed down Boston for the rest of the afternoon as our team clawed its way back against their twenty-five-game winner, Mel Parnell, until finally, with the shadows lengthening across the field, a former pitcher named Johnny Lindell sent a ball arcing high into the upper deck in left, putting the Yankees ahead 5–4. Now I know you went to games to indulge me, Ben. You didn't normally get excited, but this time, I swear, you did (even though something at the back of my mind reminds me that a rabbi's son shouldn't swear if there's any question as to which holy book is being sworn on, or danger of taking "the name of the Lord thy God in vain"). What a game! we cried to each other as the place went wild. What a game! You're as much a part of that memory in my mind as DiMaggio. I didn't know where you'd been and couldn't then imagine that you'd be leaving. The important thing was that we were there together.

5

POSSIBLY INVOLVED

Constant reference to *Good Infield Play* by Lou Boudreau hadn't made me a good infielder. *How to Play Better Tennis* by Bill Tilden had given me some useful tips about footwork on the court and the service toss, but its clear precepts on the backhand had registered only in my mind, not on my nervous system; by the time the message was sent to my right arm, the ball was already skipping by. So my faith in manuals should have been drained by the time I came upon *How to Win an Argument with a Communist* by Ray W. Sherman in the library I haunted on West 100th Street. Yet I seized on the book instantly; this one, my instincts told me, just might work. Besides, I really needed it. It was autumn 1950: roughly six months after my bar mitzvah; four months after North Korea, in the first flush of the Kim dynasty's despotism, poured across the 38th Parallel and plunged us back into war; not even two months after the start of the ninth grade at the Booker T. Washington Junior High School on Columbus Avenue. We were in a period that would be known as the McCarthy era, a time of blunderbuss accusations in which the reality of treason by persons leading double lives offered an excuse for hunting infiltrators anywhere. But my classmate and pal David Zipser, with whom I'd been having a running ideological argument, remained completely unfazed, as sublimely sure of his faith as any apostle about to be lashed to a stake. I was making no headway with him at all.

David's parents had no chance to infiltrate anything, for they were the opposite of clandestine in their allegiance to the Communist Party. Not being masked, they could never be unmasked. That was the basis for his irritating self-assurance. His advantage in debate was that he could always throw me off-balance with an accusation of "Red-baiting." His disadvantage was that he didn't care all that deeply about the politics in which he'd been raised. He found the *Daily Worker*, let alone party tracts, boring to the point of being unreadable. *Popular Mechanics* had a much firmer grip on his imagination. I felt a need to outdo and outlast him in our dialectical exercises but didn't know nearly enough. If I asked him whether workers in the Soviet Union really believed they had a voice in "the dictatorship of the proletariat," he'd tie me up in knots and leave me stammering—or worse, saying things I couldn't quite believe—by asking whether I could name a single democratic right enjoyed by voteless black sharecroppers in the segregated South. In this way, our debates became barrages of tit-for-tat rhetorical questions. Almost always, it seemed to me, he had the last word.

My memories of this period have always seemed clear, but now that two garrulous old guys, David and I, have had our reunion in La Jolla, I have to admit that those memories were shot full of errors over sequence and chronology; that they must have been willfully rearranged and censored by me for the purpose, or so I'm now inclined to postulate, of keeping ideology as far removed as possible from my gauzy, loving memories of Ben Lowell. In fact, I've no memory at all of ever hearing Ben say a word about Communism or the Soviet Union or his own political life after Montgomery, which is remarkable since Ben doesn't appear to have been particularly reserved on those topics. The historian Howard Sachar, Abe Sachar's son, recalls meeting Ben in California just before his return to New York and hearing him rail against the Marshall Plan as an American capitalist scheme to monopolize European markets. "It was such dull-witted agitprop," Howard Sachar said, "that at first I thought he was joking." My brother David, four years younger than I, remembers Ben holding forth on the wonders of Soviet health care at a reception for a visiting Oxford scholar in our Riverside Drive living room, on how the best modern care was guaranteed and free for every last worker. My dad moved in quickly to shoo David to the other end of the room as if the conversation were too risqué for his young ears. The memory boy also remembers that evening: the upswept lapels of the visitor's suit and his white-on-black polka-dot tie, his chewy accent, the way he parted his hair in the middle so that it added a slick, boldface circumflex to his forehead, the sense that he hadn't bathed—but nothing at all about anything Soviet.

What comes to mind as a transfixing moment on the ideological divide involved Arthur Zipser, David's self-contained and handsome father, who was said to be a photographer. I can picture the angle of the armchair in which he was sitting as I walked through their living room on 115th Street and Riverside in failing late afternoon light. In that picture, Mr. Zipser wears a khaki shirt. Did he catch me eyeing his copy of the *Daily Worker*? Or did I venture some comment? I can't be sure now of what he was responding to; I just remember the response. "You'll be one too," he remarked casually with a small and confident, maybe smug, smile. His point seemed to be that the ineluctable course of history would allow even me to make my contribution to the building of a classless society.

I once might have considered this encounter a catalyst in my lunge for *How to Win an Argument with a Communist*. But if I did, my timing would have been off again: the book wasn't published until the middle of 1950, nearly two years after David and his family had given up that apartment. I'd forgotten, till David reminded me in La Jolla, that his family had moved to Long Beach, California, in 1949 and that he'd disappeared from my life for the better part of a year. When the Zipsers moved back, David rejoined our class but his parents no longer lived in our neighborhood. Thereafter they lived way uptown near Dykman Street in an apartment I never visited while he stayed with an aunt and uncle downtown. So I have to backdate the occasion on which his dad acquainted me with the concept of historical inevitability. Like the date of Bobby Schoenfeld's bar mitzvah, this tiny and obscure clue serves as a warning that a virus has invaded my memory. I can no longer say what factor or combination of factors was turning me into a premature anti-Communist in the ninth grade. It could have been the strident polemics and cold logic of the period. Or on some vector formed as well by my longing to stay aligned with my dad, it could even have been our breach with Ben.

What's clear, once again, is how much escaped me as I picked my way through adolescence and my little world, how many layers of the life around me remained unimagined by me. For instance, while I knew that Arthur and Pearl Zipser, David's parents, were in the party, I had no idea till my reunion with my old friend of how fully involved they were, how closely tied to its leadership. Arthur Zipser, it turns out, was David's stepfather. His actual father, a Communist leader named Harry Gannes, had died of a brain tumor when David was three. Gannes had been a founder of the Young Communist League and the *Daily Worker*'s leading writer on foreign affairs, the propagandist who had to perform the party's pirouettes, sidesteps, and somersaults at the time of the Nazi-Soviet pact. He wrote a book on China and another on Spain before sinking into a comatose state in a darkened room on Bank Street in the first apartment David can remember. I didn't know it then, but Arthur Zipser's main occupation when David and I became friends wasn't photography but party work; specifically, manning a small branch office a few blocks from our school, a couple of flights up on Broadway with the party's name, or maybe just the initials CPUSA, painted on the window facing the street. David also never told me back then that his uncle was one of the eleven Communist leaders convicted in 1949 for "conspiracy to teach and advocate the overthrow of the government by force and violence," a slippery phrase that nearly turned teaching and advocacy into synonyms for violence. Arthur Zipser would become amanuensis to William Z. Foster, the leader of the party's hardest-line faction and author of *Toward Soviet America*, a Depression-era tract interpreting the gospel according to Lenin for American believers. Arthur would ultimately become Foster's adoring biographer, offering scant apologies, only a terse acknowledgment of Stalin's "tragic weaknesses." If a recurring tendency to mass murder was one of them, it wasn't mentioned in *Working-class Giant* when it finally appeared in 1981, twenty years after Foster's death in Moscow and ten years before the collapse of the Soviet Union, which Arthur and Pearl lived to see, their faith intact.

Now that's some heritage. As the white-haired neuroscientist talks about it today, he sounds as if he was raised in a cult. "I was really brainwashed," he says when I tell him how struck I always was by his seeming serenity. Now I'm struck as we compare memories by what he has retained about me from those years of our early adolescence. He remembers me as earnestly seeking to deprogram him; in his memories, our arguments get heated but never rancorous. He remembers how widely I was reading, mentioning titles I'd all but forgotten. He mentions my bar mitzvah, the only time he was ever in a synagogue in his life (though the gated condo development in La Jolla he enters in his Toyota Avalon with a touch on an electronic remote is practically in the shadow of one). Best of all, as far as I'm concerned, he remembers my jump shot. No one else I know could connect me to any form of athletic prowess.

David Zipser also remembers that our debates took place on Broadway and Riverside Drive as we walked back to school after lunch, which he would take at my house, bringing his own liverwurst sandwich. I remember them taking place on Morningside Drive. We're discussing two routes, two different schools, two different years.

Perhaps we're both right. The date on *How to Win an Argument with a Communist* seems to prove that we were still at it in the autumn of 1950. I had to go to the Library of Congress to find a copy of the old manual. As I turned its pages, I tried to recall what use I had made of it. Chapter 25, just a page and a half, entitled "Ask the Communist to Answer 'Yes' or 'No,'" rang a faint bell. A list of sample questions is laid out:

> *Under Communism would the nation's chief executive be a dictator?*
>
> *Under Communism, if the people became dissatisfied with the nation's chief executive, could a majority of them vote him out of office?*
>
> *Under Communism, if I wished to quit my job here and get one in another city, could I do so without government permission?*
>
> *Under Communism, would radio, television, newspapers and magazines be censored by the government?*

Could it be that I started pounding David with yes-or-no questions that autumn? Could it be that my truculence on politics finally drove us apart at a time when, ever more urgently, we had started to talk and dream about girls? We both agree that we were no longer pals by the time we went to high school the next autumn. Then, six weeks into that semester, David switched schools and vanished from my life. I've a memory of seeing him at my end of a subway car a year or so later and of our both turning away with blank stares as if we hadn't recognized one another. At least I think it's a memory. It's also possible I made it up for a lightly fictionalized account of our friendship and falling-out that I turned into a column for my high school newspaper. Not long after the column appeared it dawned on me that it had been unpleasantly sanctimonious; the thought that David might have seen it made me wince. (He said he hadn't when I finally asked him in La Jolla, leaving me with a sense that a tiny weight of shame had been lifted off my chest.) In his own recounting, David never became what you might call a convert. Politics continued to bore him. It meant mimeographing and carrying signs. On the other hand, square dances under the auspices of youth leagues of the left were good places to meet girls. He never thought that Communists could set off a nuclear war since the Communists he knew talked and talked about peace as they were directed to do in that period. But they also talked and talked about the Soviet Union, which interested him not at all. Along the way, as he moved from microbiology to neuroscience, from the East Coast to the West, and from a first marriage to a second, with a long-term relationship intervening, David found it convenient to position himself as disillusioned with all politics and wryly detached; not so different a posture, I find myself thinking, from that which a seen-it-all, above-the-fray journalist adopts as an anticreed.

If I'm right in settling on October 1950 as the month I started to use my anti-Communist manual to wind up my running debate with David Zipser, that begs new questions about what else was going on that month in my little life and the world at large. I remember a few things, none bearing on the fate of nations (though that was the month Chinese forces started slipping into North Korea, where they would soon surprise and stun General MacArthur's overextended troops).

For instance, I had to go to court to testify against several boys who had robbed me, my brother, and a friend of his in Riverside Park late in the summer as we were heading home after playing catch. (The police recovered my Rawlings mitt and the silver ID bracelet I'd made at camp but returned only the mitt, which thereafter had a stamp on the thumb that said it was the property of the court.) I remember our alleged IG (for "intellectually gifted") class being drilled on a little book called *Thirty Days to a More Powerful Vo-cabulary* so that we'd ace the competitive exam for the elite public high schools. And I remember that some of the girls in my class, who were beginning to display gifts other than intellect, asked if my parents would allow us to hold the first girl-boy party of the season in our spacious apartment. My parents' idiosyncratic bedroom, dis-guised as a den with its toe-to-toe beds made up like studio couches, became the necking room. Someone flicked off the lights, and when they went back on after a few minutes, I was startled to see one of the friskier girls on my mom's bed under one of the less bashful boys. I then learned the meaning of horny, though I'd yet to hear the word. This new preoccupation may be indirectly related to a dis-cernible sag in my interest in the World Series—the Yankees swept the Phillies in four—and my fading appetite for going to football or basketball games that autumn. (In fact, forty years would pass be-fore I next went to a Knicks game.) If I wasn't going to games, I probably wasn't seeing much of Ben Lowell, but he had to have been on my mind. After all, as I now know, October 1950 was also the month of Bobby Schoenfeld's bar mitzvah.

The provocation for Rabbi Newman's surprise attack on my dad couldn't have been the canning of Ben Lowell, as I'd long assumed it to have been, for Ben wouldn't get his final shove for another two months. Word must have been spreading in his circle that Ben was suddenly on shaky ground with my dad and Hillel for political rea-sons. Two years after reacquiring the title "rabbi," attaching it to a new name, and coming to work for my dad, he'd become conspicu-ously less inhibited about playing his old role as a clerical straight man at Communist-front functions. In March he spoke at a dinner at the Astor Hotel honoring the chairman of a front called the Joint Anti-Fascist Refugee Committee for standing up to the House Un-American Activities Committee, which then held him in contempt. In June he appeared at a Town Hall rally with seven members of the

Hollywood Ten, on the eve of their trial in Washington on contempt charges brought by the same committee. The *Times* reported the next morning that Paul Robeson put in a surprise appearance and that $10,000 had been raised for legal costs after Rabbi Benjamin Lowell made the appeal. In July he spoke at a rally in Jamaica, Queens, against a Subversive Activities Control Bill cosponsored by Representative Richard Nixon of California.

Even if the other meetings escaped his notice, the small article in the *Times* must have come to my dad's attention. It appeared on June 20, five days before the start of the Korean War. My dad was no fan of the Inquisition; he would not have needed to be told that it raised a civil liberties issue. And since Ben had worked in Hollywood, my dad might have been inclined to cut him a little slack on grounds that he had a personal stake in helping to resist the committee's assault on a passel of screenwriters. But more than likely, he'd have implored Ben to be a little careful about the sponsorship of meetings he spoke at, so as to avoid giving ammunition to a witch-hunting fringe outfit called the American Jewish League Against Communists, with which my dad had been tussling for nearly a year. Dedicated to stopping the "infiltration" of Jewish organizations by "open and disguised Communists," the league had targeted Hillel, accusing it of harboring pinko rabbis in its ranks; most prominently, in its view, Ben.

If I can see a pattern here, Ben must have seen it, too. Any appeal to Ben Lowell to be prudent would have instantly summoned to his mind the appeals made to Ben Goldstein in Montgomery seventeen years earlier when, with his job clearly on the line, he'd never hesitated about speaking at the black church in defiance of his trustees. His latent Ezekiel complex again kicked in. Two weeks after the Town Hall meeting, he spoke at the Jamaica rally; and, hurtling on, a month after that, chaired a meeting on the Korean War at a hotel called the Capital for yet another front group on the list the attorney general then kept of supposedly subversive organizations. It was in a week of orchestrated party-inspired protests against the war that largely went unnoticed, except for a small demonstration the night before in Union Square by members of Communist-led unions in which the demonstrators got clobbered by the police. This was less than six weeks after the North Korean invasion, at a point when Seoul had fallen and American and South Korean forces were still bottled up near the tip of the peninsula.

Most of the speakers in the hotel meeting room condemned the United States for interfering on behalf of a reactionary regime and for manipulating the United Nations. The Americans, in other words, were the aggressors. Rabbi Lowell was slightly less explicit politically when he rose to pass the hat. Offering himself as "not a politician"—just your regular rabbi in the street—he stopped well short of speaking for the enemy, saying in the faux folksy voice he'd adopted that he didn't like "this Korea business" and also didn't like the Americans "hiding behind the skirts of the United Nations." Then, after saying how shocked law-abiding citizens should be by the zestful exhibition of clubbing the cops had put on the previous evening in Union Square, he made his pitch, raising $500 of the $2,000 for which he pleaded. Or so an FBI informant later reported.

If the informant was there, it was not to monitor Ben. After stalking him on and off for seven years on suspicion of espionage, the FBI that summer called a time-out. The same month as the Korea meeting, the bureau's New York office put a note on Ben's ever-lengthening file: *Investigation in this case is delayed due to the fact that the agent to whom it has been assigned is and has been assigned to investigations in connection with the Julius Rosenberg, David Greenglass, Vivian Glassman, William Pearl and Morton Sobel espionage cases.* When those were over, the note promised, the stalled investigation into the Lowell espionage case, which had yielded no Soviet contacts for at least five years, would be "promptly resumed."

The mainstream press seems to have taken no notice of Ben's

appearance at an antiwar gathering. But in the prevailing climate it was only a matter of time before the finger-pointers at the American Jewish League Against Communism heard of it and pounced. That happened the week before Bobby Schoenfeld's bar mitzvah. The league's latest, sharpest denunciation of Ben, it finally becomes clear, set the stage for the clash between the two rabbis that Saturday morning. For the first time, my dad and Hillel hadn't returned the league's fire. It was that ominous silence that Rabbi Newman was denouncing when he seized on my dad's presence to put the brand of McCarthyism on Hillel. Ben, who must have been under pressure to explain himself in private, was left to offer his own defense in public. In a paper called the *National Jewish Post*, he cast himself as a victim of "insinuation, distortion, half-statement and downright inaccuracy" but failed to point out any particular error.

In rearranging the chronology, my memory had simply cast aside all the ambiguities with which that moment was suffused. My dad, who'd been championing the free expression of ideas, now found himself under pressure to conduct a purge. The former pacifist had to ask his assistant how on earth, despite his earlier assurances and the warnings he'd been given, he could mindlessly fall in step with a cynical peace campaign designed in Moscow, a throwback to the era of the Nazi-Soviet pact when believers like Ben learned to denounce "the second imperialist war."

This wasn't the sixties. Being antiwar was a constitutional right, but most Americans, five years after the defeat of the Nazis and the Japanese, were used to being on the right side in any struggle against tyranny. Being antiwar suggested a lack of patriotism and the dark tendencies so readily branded "subversive" then. Yet in my dad's eyes, Ben's real transgression was essentially personal: how could he have been so disloyal, in the narrowest sense, as to stick Hillel—and my dad—in such a corner? How much was explained to the thirteen-year-old me, how much I overheard, is unclear to me now, but my sense is not much on either score; enough for me to understand that my friend Ben would be off-limits for a while, but not enough, it seems, for me to draw any firm connection in my mind between Ben's world and Arthur Zipser's.

What would have been especially hard for my dad to swallow at this juncture was the possibility that he might eventually lose a round to another rabbi named Ben whom he'd come to see as his particular nemesis and burden that year. This was Benjamin Schultz, the mouthpiece and professional head of the American Jewish League Against Communism who'd made himself a pariah as far as organized Jewry was concerned by peddling a series of articles on the "Communist penetration of religion" in 1947 to the *World Telegram*, a soon-to-be-moribund afternoon paper that specialized in Red hunts. The second installment ran under a headline that mixed metaphors: RED CROCODILE TEARS ENSNARE SOME RABBIS. Held up as the arch example of a rabbi entangled in crocodile tears was the same Stephen S. Wise who had virtually read Ben Goldstein out of the rabbinate for aligning himself with Communists.

To a striking degree, Benjy Schultz was the mirror image of our Ben, a renegade on the right rather than the left. He had entered Wise's Jewish Institute of Religion the year our Ben graduated and had subsequently leaned on the great man for recommendations to advance his career. Then, promoting himself as a crusader, he turned on his sponsor for having been used by Communist fronts. The aging Wise, nearing the end of his life, called his former student "a professional and probably profiteering Communist-baiter." Among Wise's final words for Schultz, "mendacious" and "vicious" figured prominently. The furor that ensued eventually cost Schultz his congregation in Yonkers but led directly to the bankrolling of his tiny splinter movement by Alfred Kohlberg, a textile merchant who made his fortune between the wars by having women in south China villages embroider designs that had been sketched in Manhattan on Irish linen handkerchiefs imported from Belfast: a business plan that demonstrated a fertile imagination and nimbleness of mind, which he now applied to hunting Reds.

By the time he got involved with Schultz, Kohlberg was already the chief angel, pamphleteer, and strategist for what came to be known as "the China lobby." By some interpretations, he *was* the China lobby, the impresario behind the whole "Who lost China?" debate. It couldn't have been that Mao's Red Army had defeated Chiang Kai-shek on a surge of popular feeling, or that the rot in the Generalissimo's regime had anything to do with its collapse; he had to have been undermined and betrayed by a network of treacherous American diplomats, scholars, and journalists manipulated from Moscow. Kohlberg, who had traveled widely in China over the years and seems to have had some genuine feeling for the country, was obsessed with his mission, which was to expose them all. In this he preceded Joe McCarthy; seeking political influence, he soon became one of the senator's most stalwart backers. (Jews on the ideological right were a rarity then. That has not been the case in the last quarter century of neocon ferment and polemics. Schultz and his sponsor might be seen as pioneers.)

There's no reason to believe our Ben knew Rabbi Schultz but every reason to think that Ben Schultz in his student days had to have been aware of Ben Goldstein as a Stephen Wise favorite in the first graduating class. So perhaps in fingering Ben Lowell, Schultz imagined himself to be clinching his case against his recently deceased former mentor whom our Ben, no longer connected through marriage, hadn't dared see upon his return to New York until the great man was safely in his casket. (Stephen Wise lay in state in his synagogue on West 68th Street in April 1949. His was the first cadaver I ever saw. I filed past with a friend after a ballgame at Yankee Stadium. Ben and my dad had gone together earlier to pay their respects.) My dad felt nothing but scorn for Schultz, whom he regarded as something unclean, a vulture in human form. "Still fighting the battle of the *Schultzjuden* but that too goes well," he wrote optimistically to my mom at the start of 1950 when, as a companion to a wealthy widow, she was making her first trip to Europe. He made it sound as if he were referring to a different species of Jew.

If anything, my dad seems to have spent more time than usual outside the office with our Ben while my mom was getting used to the comforts of the Plaza-Athénée in Paris. His letters show that he brought Ben home to family dinners and roped him into accompanying us to sabbath services at a Washington Heights temple. They played tennis at Columbia and I went along to watch. Like Bill Tilden on the cover of his "how to" book, Ben wore long white trousers and displayed a graceful backhand. Obviously, the *Schultzjuden* hadn't come between them yet. When they finally did, months later, it was Alfred Kohlberg who wrote and dispatched a well-aimed letter to Frank Goldman, a lawyer from Lowell, Massachusetts, who as president of B'nai Brith exercised oversight and budgetary control of Hillel. Kohlberg's letter brought to light Ben's appearance at the Communist-front gathering against the war. "We ask whether Jewish youth is not in danger, through your instrumentality, when it is subjected to the guidance of a Benjamin Lowell," the letter said. Goldman didn't react calmly. He pressed for the issue to be taken up with urgency by my dad's board, known as the Hillel Commission, and later threatened, according to Kohlberg, to name a judge from the Court of Appeals in New York to investigate Ben if the commission failed to act.

After that, my dad seemed to be sore at both Ben and Goldman. He may have lost confidence in Ben, even to the point of concluding he had to go. At the same time, he seems to have found it hard to discharge Ben for exercising his First Amendment rights in a seedy hotel meeting room where, though he was happy to be used, he'd been coy rather than forthright in declaring his views. What he'd actually said could have been said aloud in any diner or tavern in America, where it would have been taken as a nativist muttering against foreigners in general, not the Everyman version of the Communist line. It was the platform from which he spoke and what the other speakers had said that lent his words a slightly sinister edge. His performance had been devious, as was his connection to a shadowy network that continued to find him useful. But did this justify sacking him? And if it really mattered so much, how could you figure out whether he was a naïve fellow traveler or disciplined party member? Ben's own answers, in their vagueness and evasiveness, pointed both ways.

The fact that Ben wasn't immediately fired seems to suggest that someone, I'd like to think my dad, was making an argument that it would set a dangerous precedent, that the removal of one rabbi would lead to demands for the purge of others. It could also be seen as capitulation to Kohlberg and Schultz, as an admission that they'd been right. What then was my dad going to say when he had the impulse to rise and face the indignant Newman at Bobby Schoenfeld's bar mitzvah? Could he have said that his organization believed in the Bill of Rights, believed in its staff, and wouldn't run loyalty checks or limit its right of free expression?

He must have felt, as he leaned forward and grasped the pew in front of us till his knuckles whitened, that he could speak in some such terms; otherwise he'd have known he had nothing much to say to rebut Newman's charge of McCarthyism. But if he'd allowed himself to sound so lofty, he might have had to work in a little escape clause. He might have had to suggest what could happen if the organization ceased to believe in a member of its staff. For that's where my dad and Abe Sachar, his commission chairman and by now president of Brandeis University, found themselves with Ben, whose assertions of political independence no longer rang true. If he had told them when he was hired that he wasn't presently a party member but still meant to be helpful to the cause, he probably wouldn't have been hired. Obviously, he'd said less than that, and just as obviously,

having heard him discourse in private on the wickedness of the
Marshall Plan and the wonders of Soviet health care, they thought
they'd had an understanding that whatever he was, he was now on
the sidelines; at a minimum, a gentleman's agreement about discre-
tion. Now, they found, it had expired.

What they did next was try to find out whether Ben had actually
lied to them, which you would only do, it seems to me from the distance now of more than half a century, if you were seeking a basis for
dismissal. Hillel and B'nai Brith, now separate organizations, claim
to have lost or misplaced their records from the early fifties. The FBI,
however, takes better care of its papers. A few weeks after Bobby
Schoenfeld's bar mitzvah, J. Edgar Hoover received a "Dear Ed" letter on White House stationery from David K. Niles, a presidential
assistant who signed himself "Dave." It concerned Benjamin Lowell
(who Niles appeared to think was a former rabbi) and it was
prompted, he said, by a request "from my friend President Sachar of
Brandeis University."

Niles, a Bostonian from a family of Russian Jewish immigrants
originally named Neyhus, was a holdover from the Roosevelt White
House serving as Truman's special assistant for minorities. Consistently liberal and discreetly Zionist, he had opened the door to the
Oval Office for Zionist pleaders like my dad. Robert J. Donovan, a
Truman biographer, credits him with keeping "the case for Zionism
before Truman." He also was not above a bit of bowing and scrap-
ing when he thought it might be helpful. "I wish that some of our
friends would ask our advice before they commit themselves," his
letter to Hoover begins. It then introduces Ben, tells a bit about his
background, and poses the problem:

> Now, the heads of the Hillel Foundation have become worried
> about Mr. Lowell, and they have asked me if I could confi-
> dently [sic] find out if he is someone they should retain on

their staff. I think enough of the Hillel Foundation to want to save them, if possible, even from their own indiscretions. Please tell me what to advise them.

If I'd come upon this letter at age thirteen, I'd have considered it a striking lesson on how the world sometimes works. Now that I'm at a much later stage in life, I should be less surprised, but my eyebrows are probably raised higher than that boy's would have been. On its face, the White House aide seemed to be asking the nation's top cop to decide whether a rabbi was kosher. But is that really what Sachar and my dad had wanted or had something got lost in translation? Had they wanted facts by which to test the truth of what Ben had told them about his politics past and present? Or had they wanted to offload the responsibility for judging Ben onto the government?

What's fascinating is to see how skillfully Hoover avoids overstepping his professional brief, at least on paper. The director sends along a single-spaced memo of slightly more than four pages with a summary of assorted gleanings from Ben's fat file but sidesteps Niles's invitation to turn thumbs up or down. More striking than what's in the memo is what's left out. It never says that the bureau had little or no interest in what Ben actually believed, that it had been investigating him for seven years on suspicion of *espionage*, and that it had reason to think he had contact with the KGB station chief for the whole United States. (Hoover might not have known Zubilin's role in early 1943 or that the Russian may have learned about the real purpose of the Manhattan Project before anyone thought it necessary to brief the director of the FBI. But by 1950 he'd have had a retrospective grasp of his rival's accomplishments.) The omission could have been based on a scruple; Ben, after all, hadn't been connected to any particular plot. Given the mood of the times, such fastidiousness seems a fairly remote possibility. More likely the omission may have been due to the inherent difficulty of distilling a thick FBI file, which could also be why the memo neglected to mention the report that Ben had been expelled from his party branch in Beverly Hills in 1948. What the memo did appear to establish was that he'd been a party member in California for five or so years. Hoover's covering letter to Niles offered no judgment at all on Ben Lowell, not even to the extent of saying the record speaks for itself.

The White House aide phoned the director the next day, ostensibly to ask whether the memo could be shown to Sachar and my dad, but really, it seems, to negotiate the terms of a verdict. In a note he dictated to his aides and the file, Hoover told how the conversation went. He indicated to Niles that it would be better if the memo were not sent on. "Mr. Niles then stated he understood," the note said, "and would therefore just tell the President [*sic*] of the Foundation that the sooner they get rid of this individual the better it would be, and that . . . he, Niles, is against his retention." The words are attributed to Niles but it's not a great stretch to imagine that they could originally have been Hoover's. So that's how it was done. Niles, who'd had a hand in recruiting Abe Sachar to Brandeis, invites Hoover to visit the school. "I told him the next time I was out that way I would certainly try to stop by," the director's note concludes.

Niles then passes on the quasi-official sooner-the-better verdict from the White House. How much more than the verdict he relayed is unclear but Sachar and my dad appear to have taken whatever they were told as the final word, proving that Ben had been less than truthful about his commitments and therefore wasn't trustworthy. They were in the tricky, sometimes perilous position of reporters dealing with official sources who speak, as newspapers now say, "on condition of anonymity," providing their own gloss on some bit of intelligence or record they've seen rather than the thing itself. What's not clear to me, now that I've read the memo they presumably never saw, was what they could have learned that they hadn't already known. When Ben had told Sachar back in California that he was not a party member, did Sachar take him to mean that he'd never been one? It was on this fine distinction that any estimate of his candor and veracity depended.

Of course, what I'm really looking for in this ancient and obscure saga—the sort of subhistory that's never likely to be explored—is a vantage point from which to view my dad and, through him, the person I was then becoming. If, as now seems likely, J. Edgar Hoover and David Niles had as much to do with the verdict on Ben as my dad or Abram Sachar, who ostensibly made it, I can begin to understand why my dad seemed so conflicted and unhappy that weekend in December 1950 when the whole affair finally came to a head. I've a picture in my mind of him coming home late for dinner and my trying to ask him questions as he hung up his tie and jacket and went through his ritual of emptying his pockets and arraying his money clip, cigarette case, and watch chain on top of the bureau in the foyer. In that picture, his countenance, which tended to beam, is drawn and his jaws are locked, signaling he's in no mood to talk. My mom pulls me aside and whispers that my dad is feeling pressure because Ben is being made to resign.

It's a memory that never found its place in the jigsaw puzzle I'd built around Bobby Schoenfeld's bar mitzvah; it just didn't fit. Now, on the basis of inference from a larger body of facts, I think I've an idea of where that piece might go. I think my dad found himself in the position of having to choose between a colleague he could no longer trust and an impenetrable quasi-official finding he was asked to take on faith. And there was no putting off the choice. That Ben hadn't deviated from the party line for something like fifteen years was a fact, but it wasn't a new fact. Whether he had been a party member in recent years was an obscure and possibly meaningless question since, of course, he would have understood that he couldn't openly be a member and function as a rabbi: Stephen Wise had taught him that much. But in the climate of 1950 it happened to be the question of the hour, on which everything had to be made to turn. Yet the FBI, which had helped shape the conclusion that the sooner he was gone the better, hadn't even addressed it. No one said a word about his actual performance in his job. Ben was hauled before the Hillel Commission's personnel committee (which included a University of Michigan professor, a former president of Queens College, an Orthodox rabbi, Abe Sachar, and my dad). Functioning as a Star Chamber, they asked for an answer on the issue of party membership. The answers they got were not forthright. They split hairs over dates and definitions. Ben did a bob and weave. He was told it would be in the best interests of Hillel if he resigned. No announcement was made.

My dad, it now turns out, had drafted an announcement that camouflaged the real reasons behind a screen of the usual pro forma regrets over Ben's departure; it said he'd rendered exceptional service. Abe Sachar stripped off the regrets and regard. "I know how important the amenities are," Sachar wrote my dad in what was for him an unusually sharp memo. But courtesy would be wasted on Ben Lowell. "I feel that he betrayed our confidence in him and let us down very badly. He gave explicit promises that Hillel interests would come first and he lied about his previous associations." The draft, Sachar chided my dad, reflected "the kindness of your heart, but I wouldn't count it as good judgment."

If Sachar or my dad had been familiar with the sequence of events in Montgomery, they'd have known what to expect. Ben got his story out first. He told a Jewish news service that Kohlberg's "half-truths" and "insinuations" had created "a turmoil of fear" in the organization, and that the commission needed to sacrifice him for the sake of public relations. The Jewish papers appeared weekly so my dad's reply didn't get printed till after New Year's Day. The acceptance of Ben's resignation, his statement said defensively, "was not motivated by the charges of any outside individual or any outside group and certainly not by considerations of what might prove to be expedient from the standpoint of public relations." Hillel would stand behind any member of its staff "who deserves protection against irresponsible charges." That seemed to say loud and clear that our Ben had not deserved protection against "irresponsible charges." The clumsy wording is another clue that my dad wasn't comfortable, after all, with the way it had played out. Perhaps he wouldn't have been so ready with a reply to the censorious Newman if that scene in the synagogue had really come after Ben's departure, as I'd long made myself think. Taking my cues from my dad, it seems I switched the chronology in order to place him in a time when he could be full of spirit and fight.

The experience may have left my dad with something of a bad taste in his mouth, but he was never given to brooding on the past. I doubt that he thought much about Ben after banishing him. From time to time over the years I'd mention my interest in Ben Lowell. My dad would react as if I'd mentioned the name of one of Bonaparte's ministers or, perhaps, a minor poet he'd heard of but never read. It was faintly interesting that I was interested. It was clear that he wasn't. I didn't press him because I thought I had the sequence of events straight. But in rearranging things, I'd misplaced the fact that a full two months had passed between revelation of the Korea meeting and Ben's departure; and I'd never known how guarded Ben's words there had been or that, finally, J. Edgar Hoover himself had been consulted. I always believed that my dad had acted on clear principles. Now I don't think that's how it felt to him. Ben had put him in a situation where he ended up closer to the position of the witch-hunters than he ever imagined he could find himself. It was Ben who had stuck him there, sure, but then what's freedom of speech for if it only belongs to those who'll always be beyond reproach in the use they make of it? If I'm right, my dad would have claimed only to have made the best of a bad situation. And since this, clearly, was not the way I wanted to remember it, I remembered it another way.

I also didn't want to know, or ever have to remember, that my

parents' marriage was again on the rocks. I had my own room with
a door I could shut, so I shut that out, too. I was free to come and
go whenever I wanted; if storm clouds started to gather around my
mom, I mostly went, usually to play ball in the park. My avoidance
strategy was already taking shape. Its purpose was to make sure
that any renewed hints of dissolution in our household would not
get through to unsettle me. But the old camp trunk contained evidence that Ben Lowell was a distant second on my dad's list of problems in 1950. The low point seemed to come a week to the day after
my bar mitzvah in April, when my mother renewed old accusations
of infidelity against my dad and demanded a divorce. Such a sun-
dering had come up before as an option but never, as far as I can tell,
as a demand. On that Saturday, as my dad stood by the door of their
bedroom with his bag packed, about to leave on a trip, my distraught
mom said something stinging, truly breathtaking, to demonstrate
the futility of trying to mend what was torn. Wherever we were at
that moment, their sons had no idea how near a precipice they were.
Echoes of what may have been said that Saturday didn't begin to
reach us for many years, after our parents had finally gone their separate ways and we had embarked on ours. By his own account, my
dad went reeling out the door. Yet it couldn't have taken longer than
a couple of hours for him to convince himself that he had to fight
for the marriage, once again.

His initial response, written on a flight to Pittsburgh hours later
as a five-point brief in favor of a marriage in tatters, voices pain, determination, and abiding love. It's beyond fathoming by his eldest son,
I have to admit, but there's something in it, a quality neither self-
denying nor self-effacing, that comes across as unforced and stoic in
the best sense of the word; he was not pure or innocent, just too
worn down to be anything but himself. To my surprise, I find myself
wanting to call that quality nobility. He's "smarting," he says, and
"afraid to expose myself to new humiliation." But separation holds

no promise of happiness for either of them. "So," he writes, "I think we had better turn and face one another." He vows to resist a divorce, testifies that he has "a yearning and a capacity for fidelity," then concludes: "I want to love you and no one else, and, if it's not too late, I want you to love me and no one else." Ten days later, still on the road and still pleading, he writes, "Pride is only a word."

My mom's dream of breaking free didn't soon subside. She was about to collect her doctorate at thirty-eight and now wanted to step down from her Hillel job at Hunter College as well as her marriage to make a new start. In November, on the day J. Edgar Hoover dispatched his memo on Ben to the White House, she sent a typed business letter to my dad as national director of the organization, declaring her intention to leave. She wasn't able to make good on that desire for another six years, presumably because my dad, who was always hard up and looking for new ways to "consolidate our debts," convinced her that the loss of her meager salary would cause our failing family fortunes to fall through the floor. Since her extravagance was an obvious cause of our chronic indebtedness, she was again trapped. In a job she wanted to leave and a marriage she was at least intermittently interested in ending, my mom found lots of reasons to rail against what she would characterize as hypocrisy. For reasons that were not specifically political, she had come to find Ben Lowell a sympathetic figure at exactly the moment he was being turned into an outcast. Whatever the nature of his nonconformity, he hadn't conformed and now he was having to start all over. It was what, in a very different way, she thought she wanted to do, so he appeared to her almost heroic in his going.

She would describe him as having been supremely self-assured but impersonal, "not in the least flirtatious." It was a personality she had previously found "alien," yet she quietly sided with him at the time of his ouster and apparently let him know it. "I can scarcely express my disappointment in Daddy's incapacity for steadfastness," she wrote in a reminiscence about Ben when she was nearly seventy-five. She plainly meant my dad's lack of steadfastness in relation to herself as well as his colleague. All in all, that seemed to me a very odd way for my mom to look at Ben's case, not to mention her own; the analogy she seemed to be drawing between her desire to break free and Ben's ouster would have occurred only to her. But then any truism we utter about the impossibility of knowing what has gone on in a marriage must apply exponentially to the marriages of which we are the issues.

My dad never saw Ben again. My mother saw him twice and so did I. The first time was about a month after his ouster when he showed up at our apartment on a Sunday night, my dad being out of town yet again, to take my mom out to dinner. I was sprawled in my dad's yellow leather chair by the window in the big room we called "the study," reading. On a winter night, the wind off the river would probably have been rattling the panes of the storm windows. Ben sauntered across the adjoining foyer, past the open double doors, tossing me the slightest of nods. He was wearing a blazer and slacks, and seeing him from the side, I was struck again by the broadness of his shoulders. Even more so, I was struck, to the point of being immobilized, by his apparent lack of interest in me. I had been used to having his eyes fasten on me. Never before had he seemed dismissive. It was as if a rope had been stretched across the entrance to the room, fixing the distance between us. Only now do I ask myself why I failed to get out of the chair to greet him and how he must have interpreted this after all the weeks, or months, we'd been out of touch. It was as if staying in my dad's chair, I stayed on my dad's side of the fence.

My mother's last meeting with Ben came about half a year later. Before noon on a summer morning, as she later recalled, he simply showed up on the path leading to a cabin in the woods my parents were renting in Putnam County. He'd spent the previous months

working in the promotion department of a publishing house. And he'd just been fired by a small congregation in Elmhurst where he'd begun moonlighting during his time at Hillel. The congregation voted 76–50 against renewing his contract, according to the *World Telegram*, on more or less the same charges of ties to "listed" organizations that had eventually caught up with him at Hillel. It was his second scalping at the hands of Ben Schultz and it came just a month after the FBI's New York office notified headquarters, in a small spasm of bureaucratic recklessness, that it was shutting down the long-pending Ben Lowell espionage case on grounds that the investigation had failed to show that "the subject is engaged in espionage activity." Washington wouldn't hear of it, perhaps because the director had now shown an interest; the case was promptly reopened.

Somehow Ben scrambled to safe ground. He'd gotten an offer from a Reform Jewish congregation that was ostensibly beyond the reach of the American Jewish League Against Communism and the FBI. It was in the steamy Havana of Fulgencio Batista and Ernest Hemingway, pre-Castro Havana, and it was known locally as the Templo Reformita. Dating from the American occupation after the Spanish-American War, it was the oldest Jewish congregation on the island, inhabiting a former mansion that had previously been the premises of the Anglo-American Women's Club; services were conducted mainly in English and mainly for Americans, many of whom had lived their whole lives there in what amounted to a colonial setting. That was what Ben, whose creed ought to have made him a staunch anticolonialist, had come to tell my mother. "We embraced and wept and didn't say another word," my mom wrote.

I was the last one in my family to see Ben. That was a year and a half after he'd established himself in Cuba, when he suddenly had to return to New York for major surgery. By then the FBI, now following him through the office of the legal attaché in the American Embassy, had already been informed that Ben had "quite a following among the Jewish community in Havana, especially among the younger people whom he seems to have impressed very much." What impressed them was the same blend of downright skepticism about matters theological and provocative thinking in the public sphere that had won Ben Goldstein a following in Montgomery twenty years earlier, only now that he was offshore, the Havana Ben was less inclined than ever before to muffle his views. An informant, possibly a member of the congregation, wrote a memo for the embassy calling for "a close and longer observation of the strange 'rabbi.'" Only Ben's looseness of lip keeps him from concluding, the memo writer says, that the rabbi must be a clandestine Communist leader in an unlikely disguise. The writer offers a small anthology of Ben's stray remarks. They stray very far, adding up to a rant. Ben argues that the arms industry instigated the Korean War to block a disarmament proposal for which the Soviet Union was ready; that there's no real democracy or free expression in the United States; and that Americans are spiritually and ideologically backward. Asked about mass murder in Stalin's Russia, he replies, so the memo says, "And how many have been killed in the United States?"

Yet addressing his own daughter at about the same time, the strange rabbi is less strange and notably more rabbinic. Jo Rogers, the former Josie Stern, née Josephine Goldstein, has saved a single letter from her dad, written from Havana at the end of 1951, the closest thing she has to a testament. "Dearest Josie," he types, and goes on to fill both sides of the page, single-spaced, till he has to complain about his arthritic fingers. "Love, Ben," it's then signed. Surprisingly, it's Judaism on which the rabbi wants to dwell, not just his notion of Judaism as a "civilization" or culture rather than a religion but Judaism as history and a set of values that he hopes she'll consider delving into. He sends her a lecture he gave at the University of Havana and refers her to an essay by a noted historian. Not only that, he urges her to make contact with the chief of the Jewish collection at the New York Public Library, a historian named Joshua Block with whom he has apparently been friendly. Ben acknowledges that he has had little to do with the nurturing of his daughter, now an undergraduate at a small Indiana college. He seems almost to dream in the middle of the Havana night that the librarian might fill in for him. "I'd like him to know you," he writes. Not quite an apology, it's a timorous letter of introduction to his daughter from the father he wishes he had been and seems to come from some place colder and farther away than Havana, from the wintry heart of his own solitude perhaps.

In the Moscow exile he'd have chosen if he'd had his way, he presumably would not have been a rabbi; more likely a small cog in some propaganda machine. Unsurprisingly, that single letter to Josie from an exile where he was freer to be his divided self failed to form the basis of a new relationship with his daughter. So when he was laid up in Manhattan fifteen months later following his surgery, he still had that unfinished, barely started, life task before him. It seems he didn't feel equal to it, for he told his ever-loyal first wife, Margaret Stern (by then circulation manager of the liberal, strenuously anti-Communist biweekly *The Reporter*), that he didn't want her to bring their daughters to the hospital to see him when she came to deliver the pajamas, toiletries, magazines, and mysteries she had gathered for him.

He didn't want to see their daughters but he was more than happy to see me. That's a paradox of which I was completely unaware at the time. I can only think of two explanations now. One is that I was less important and so didn't confront him with a sense of failure and a challenge to which he felt he would be unable to rise. The other is that he may have wanted me to remember him as a friend and not as the rabbi my dad had fired; if anything, my loyalty may have had an added value because I was the son of the man who'd banished him. Or maybe I'm now thinking too hard over an unbridgeable distance in time.

What I know is that there was no awkwardness in our reunion at Beth Israel Hospital downtown on a blustery Sunday afternoon in March. Ben sat on the edge of his hospital bed and we chatted for the better part of an hour as if we'd never fallen out of touch. It was a week or two after the death of Stalin, an event that must have reverberated in my friend's consciousness, but I've no recollection that it was even mentioned. If I brought it up, it would have been only to test Ben's reaction, but I was not in a testing mood. I was too happy to be in his company again.

I was then a high school junior, a few weeks from my sixteenth birthday, starting to think about college. That's the sort of thing adults would ask about, so maybe Ben did. And maybe he talked about the good life in Havana to which he said he'd be returning soon. What I remember is that he showed me the dressing on his incision, boasted about the huge scar he would have, and proudly informed me that, according to his surgeon, he'd just been relieved of the largest spleen in medical history. It weighed twelve pounds, he said. This was nothing to boast about. In a man Ben's age, a greatly enlarged spleen most likely points to cancer, leukemia, or lymphoma. If Ben had any inkling of a prognosis, it didn't show in his face or manner. He still looked robust and cheerful.

Not quite fifty-three, he died three months later in Mount Zion Hospital in San Francisco, with his sisters and brothers close at hand. He had managed to stay in Havana for scarcely a month, living in the spacious home of the congregation's president, near a golf course in the upscale Miramar section, before it became apparent that his condition was worsening. Then he flew to Miami en route to California, knowing by then that he was going home to die. This time Josie and Linda were given a green light to fly to California to see their father. Ben no longer looked robust; by now he was wan and wasted. The two young women wanted to return to the hospital for a second visit but their elusive, difficult father nixed it, saying he didn't want them to remember him the way he then looked. The strongest, warmest memory of Ben with which Josie was then left was of roughhousing with him on the floor of their Los Angeles home years before when she was eight or nine, with her mother standing to the side warning, "Someone's going to get hurt." That, the letter from Havana, and $1,419.61 (enough to pay for a year's college tuition back then) were the sum of her inheritance.

The FBI had fired off teletypes as Ben made his way from Miami to the West Coast and recorded his death the day after it happened. Even after his cremation, the bureau continued to comb his file for clues. The last report was compiled in October 1954, sixteen months after he died. The bureau's epitaph was not poetic. SUBJECT'S FREQUENT ASSOCIATION WITH ALLEGED NKVD AGENTS, one of the last teletypes said, STRONGLY INDICATES THAT SUBJECT WAS POSSIBLY INVOLVED

IN SOVIET ESPIONAGE IN THE PAST. If they had tried for pithiness or summary judgment, "possibly involved" would have been the best they could do. That would have surprised the columnist in an English-language paper in Havana who eulogized Ben as "one of the finest men ever to live at the 23rd parallel."

I've clear memories of June 1953, the month Ben died. I started smoking, beginning with a pack of Philip Morris I lifted from my dad's drawer but switching before long to Lucky Strikes. I had dates with a girl named Sue. I remember leaving her apartment late one night humming a pop song of that season called "Candy Lips," and that then I never called her again. That was gauche but summer was upon us and I was off to Maine with high hopes of a summertime romance. It didn't occur to me that autumn would inevitably follow summer and that it might be in my interest as well as common courtesy to say something like, "Let's stay in touch," or "I'll call when I get back." And I remember that, traveling on my own to Maine for the first time, I read a *Time* magazine cover story on a Texas politician named Lyndon Johnson on the Trailways bus to Portland. In Maine I got to use a chain saw, another first.

I remember all that but cannot remember how I learned of the death of my friend Ben Lowell or what I then felt. Probably I got the news before I left the city, but it's also possible that it came later in a letter from my mom and that, with no one to tell, I was left to absorb it on my own. The feelings I can't specifically recall would still have been a muddle, which is doubtless why I can't summon them up. They would have been compounded of loyalty to my dad, my contradictory reluctance to judge Ben and relief that my friendship with him had been renewed at the end. My dad's good opinion meant more to me than Ben's, but I'd understood from the first that Ben's would never be in question. (In a diary he kept on a trip to Europe in 1951, my dad's doubts about me are nicely balanced with his wish to believe that I wasn't a lost cause. He describes me as "taciturn and reserved"—he wasn't the last to think that—and goes on: "I have the impression that under the reserve there is a great deal of inner strength—I hope I'm right.") Somehow it had always been easy to be the opposite of reserved with Ben.

If anything, he'd been reserved with me, keeping me at a distance from the ideological strife that set the course of his life. I wouldn't have thought then what I can't help thinking now, that I was living closer than I knew to the crosscurrents of that time, an adolescent finding his footing at just a couple of removes from history. If Ben had lived, he might have used up my affection; the temptation to judge him could easily have become irresistible. Much later, that nearly happened with each of my parents. Sensing their own inevitable disappointments in later years, I had the presumption to feel disappointed in them. By his early departure, Ben got to be unchanging. I'd never know what impression Khrushchev's speech on Stalin's crimes or the images of Soviet tanks in Budapest might have made on him. He'd been skeptical about received ideas on every subject except one. Could he have let that one go or would he have clung to his faith, like Arthur Zipser, until past the end? The alternatives seem equally improbable.

Ben, for me, became a story to be reported someday. I waited so long, the obvious judgments seem just that, obvious. He wasn't independent, he wasn't his own man, but because he'd never chosen the comfortable way, he was able to imagine that he'd been true to himself. That would have proved a diminishing consolation if he'd lived long enough. So, yes, it's very likely that I wouldn't have had much patience with him if he'd turned out to be a sanctimonious old lefty, remembering only what he'd condemned, forgetting all that he'd condoned. But since he got to be unchanging, my gratitude and love remained unchanged too.

The other Ben rates a footnote. The high point of Rabbi Benjamin Schultz's life came in April 1955 when he was honored at a testimonial dinner at which Joe McCarthy, fresh from formal censure by his peers in the U.S. Senate, gave the main address of tribute. Fund-raising dinners became the central function of the American Jewish League Against Communism after Roy Cohn, McCarthy's old counsel and hit man, took over the chairmanship Alfred Kohlberg had held. By then Ben Schultz, living out his predestined pattern as the mirror image of Ben Goldstein, had gone South on a reverse trajectory to our Ben's, landing as the rabbi in Clarksdale, Mississippi, where he would end his days. "What America needs is more Mississippi, not less," he said at a ladies' lunch, soon after his arrival. Northern preachers needed to "fight the Cold War for America, even if it means less time for them to attack the South." Not long after Schultz offered this testimony to his new neighbors, northern preachers started to head South in the cause of civil rights for blacks. One of them was my dad.

6

DEN OF LIONS

I was on an errand worthy of Hermes, messenger of Zeus. It was also the best boondoggle available to copyboys at *The New York Times*, where I worked for several months in the spring of 1960, little suspecting that I was making what's now called a life choice. The errand, as barked out by Sammy Solovitz, the tiny insomniac who supervised the copyboys, was to "go get the weather." That meant riding the subway all the way down to Rector Street—I always took the local train so as to have more time with whatever novel I was reading—and then walking over to the Weather Bureau on Battery Park Place, where I was instructed to say, "I'm from the *Times*. I've come for the weather." This was after the age of gaslight, it may be noted, but well before the advent of the Internet or fax. The weather came in the form of a mimeographed map, which was handed over in a plain brown envelope. On this particular evening, which abruptly ended my first term of employment at the paper, the Weather Bureau clerk said I needed to call home immediately. There was an emergency. My mother, my bride of ten months then informed me, was being taken by ambulance to Mount Sinai Hospital following an overdose of pills in her hotel room on the East Side. It was not clear that the hospital would be able to save her.

As I gripped the phone there in the Weather Bureau, I realized instantly that I would count myself doubly responsible if her attempt succeeded this time. First, a long, preachy letter I'd sent to my parents in Cleveland, where they'd moved nearly two years earlier, had set the stage for her sudden and desperate drive back to New York the previous day. And, second, I'd merely been puzzled, not properly alarmed, when she failed to show up as planned in the late afternoon for an early dinner at our apartment before I had to leave for work. I thought of staying home but soon persuaded myself not to over-react. When the hotel operator said there was no answer and a few other calls failed to uncover any trace of her, I thought too easily of all the ways my mom could have been detained: visiting a friend I hadn't thought to phone; in some doctor's office; getting her hair done; shopping; in traffic. Never again, for the rest of her life, would I fail to think of the most dire possibility when her phone wasn't answered at an hour I thought she should be home. One evening twenty-some years later, when she was well into her seventies, I found myself sprinting up Broadway as if being chased, only to discover, when I let myself into her apartment, that she'd fallen asleep on her good ear. But on the one occasion when she'd clearly put her life in my hands, it was her old friend and professor Maurice Valency who'd had a premonition and the basic good sense to insist that the hotel send someone into her room, where she was found in a comatose state.

I caught an express train back to Times Square—my devotion to duty seemed absurd even then but the weather had to get there in time for the first edition—and then raced by cab to Mount Sinai. It was past midnight when I went out to LaGuardia Airport to fetch my dad, who'd managed to make the last flight out of Cleveland. From the early hours of the morning to daybreak, we paced the hospital corridor, waiting for someone to say my mom was out of danger, and, when that didn't happen, filling in the time with the longest, frankest, saddest conversation the two of us would ever have. I re-member only my dad's end, which is to say I've no memory of any expression of remorse by me for the letter that had been the catalyst for my mom's collapse. But I don't see how that could have been avoided. So I hypothesize—or simply now choose to think—that my dad's despairing reflections on the futility of his efforts to keep his marriage from falling apart and make my mother believe for more than a few months at a time that it could be other than a dead end for her were his way of helping me see that I was magnifying my own role and guilt. I had to understand that this was not something new; it was his stubbornness and failure, not mine, that were now on display. I saw my dad in those hours as I'd never seen him before. He had touched bottom but he was neither indulging in self-pity nor blaming my mother. As far as I could see, he was focused entirely on one question: what might have been, might be, best for her. He was not the answer, he seemed to be saying, and quite possibly there was none. The family, as a family, didn't seem to figure in his thoughts that night.

If that's the way it went—if his ruminations were offered for my sake, to ease my sense of guilt—I got no absolution. That dark night, and ever after, the thought of my righteous letter to my parents appalled me. It didn't turn up in the old camp trunk, but I remember it as three or four pages of scribbled indignation on lined legal paper. Seldom have I been so sure of myself, so right; never have I been so disastrously right. The issue seemed deceptively simple. Would my dad's mother, a widow by then for five years, be invited to Cleveland for the Passover seder and allowed to spend a week or so with her only child in the grand and spacious house my parents had rented where the back lawn sloped down to the very shore of Lake Erie? She had been out there only once and then briefly. Not to be invited for a year and a half, to be perpetually stalled, was to be left isolated, sad, and shamed before her cousins and the friends with whom she played canasta. She was the least demanding of people, but someone had to state her claim. Such was the argument and tone of my letter—or I should say my brief—which achieved its goal: my mom relented. My dad, who could always be relied on to choose the path of least resistance—or so my mom always said—went along. A few days after Grandma's arrival, exasperated for no apparent reason—

none, at least, that I ever heard—Mom skipped town with the result we now had before us.

As my mom saw and felt it, Grandma's passivity—the finiteness, the absolute ordinariness of her expectations—stood for all the inertia, all the conventions, all the obstacles that checked her own progress on the path to the more independent life to which she felt entitled. After years of insisting that such a life could be led only in New York—to the point of causing my dad to give up his Hillel job, in which he'd thrived, when the organization moved its headquarters to Washington, insisting then that if he moved, he'd move alone—she'd made a surprisingly valiant attempt two years later to find her own way in Cleveland. In between, my dad had worked in what was essentially a fund-raising job where he proved to be unsuited to the task of buffing the egos of wealthy donors. His return to the pulpit in what was reputed then to be the largest Reform Jewish congregation in the land was the only move open to him, and this time, out of necessity but also a recognition that my dad needed to do his real work, my mom surprised herself and him by going along. Soon she had fashioned a brave new start for herself too. Western Reserve took her on as a lecturer, eventually giving her one of its sunrise semester courses on TV; its university press eagerly accepted her thesis for publication as a book. *Shylock on the Stage* appeared, finally, with a striking, overly studied jacket photo that she had commissioned by the portraitist of the great and famous, Karsh of Ottawa; it showed her looking up from her manuscript as if someone had just called out from the next room to ask how long she was going to be fussing over those pages, or wouldn't she like a sherry. All the surface signs—my mom's happy reimmersion in literature, the bright and accomplished new friends my parents were discovering, the fact that for the first time since Omaha they were sleeping in a double bed—seemed to suggest that she was finally finding a kind of balance and contentment in her life.

Until my bombshell landed, showing her, I now suppose, that she was still at cross-purposes with her family and herself. At this great distance, strangely enough, it's easier for me to figure out my mother's feelings than my own. Nothing was more important to me at this stage in my life—two years out of college, nearly one year into my own marriage—than staking out my tenuous independence from my parents. As I then conceived it, this was mainly a matter of not taking money from them because they gave it so grudgingly. My dad had made it a point of honor for me to earn a major portion of my college expenses, which I'd done by working in resort hotels for tips as a busboy, chair boy, and cabana boy—any kind of "boy" these establishments had to offer. He lectured me on the inestimable value of the experience of working with my hands, on how sorry he was he'd never done it himself. As always I longed to please my parents, but over four such summers I eventually came to feel that my point of honor stood for little more than their convenience as Dad struggled to keep his "head above water," a phrase he used whenever he had to face a stack of unpaid bills. In the days when a Harvard tuition was in three or four figures rather than five, a busboy's tips accumulated over a summer could actually stretch far enough to cover it. At the end of the summer, however, I'd regularly find that some sudden urge on my mother's part had made a necessity of a luxury, leaving me to wonder why it was I'd just spent a dozen weeks impressed like an eighteenth-century seaman into a seven-days-a-week job when I might have been hiking or traveling or learning a language like many of my friends. One summer, funds were found in the family exchequer to pay for a Steinway baby grand piano in a warm walnut veneer, which then sat in our foyer as if in retirement since no one in the family brought any real accomplishment or ambition to the instrument; a well-polished symbol of our cultural aspirations is what it became. The next summer my mom fell into an opportunity on an above-average mink coat that was too good to pass up. Making such discoveries, I'd think back with carefully cultivated and preserved bitterness to my summer on a Nebraska farm and fume like my mom about the hypocrisies that curtailed my freedom. Occasionally this fuming was out loud; mostly it was in my head. (I doubt I ever said what I regularly imagined saying: "I hope you like the piano and coat I bought you.") In our first few months on our own, Carolyn and I blew every last cent we had on extended travel across Europe, from London down to the Aegean. For my part, it was a statement that I'd broken free and was finally in charge of my life, however improvidently.

So here's the question to which all this whiny antinostalgia leads: If I'd truly broken free, where did I get off giving my recently fledged self the right to blast my parents with a righteous lecture on their duties to my grandma? The answer seems obvious enough: good old displacement. I'd found a disinterested way to vent my own anger. That I'd been right on the merits wasn't much consolation as we waited through the night for the doctors to venture an opinion on my mom's condition, or later when I had to go and rouse her parents, soon after daybreak, to tell them that their eldest daughter was hovering between life and death. As I stood at the threshold of their Washington Heights apartment, my grandma, barefoot in a white nightgown, keened recriminations against her child into the hallway as if my mom were able to hear them, or as if to say she'd better recover so she could receive a proper scolding. How could she have done this to such a perfect husband, Gussie Bookholtz cried out, raising her fists in a heavenward lamentation. How patient he'd been, how he'd suffered. Involuntarily, I thought of Florence Eldridge in the third act of the original Broadway production of *Long Day's Journey into Night*, but this was no performance. Grandpa just looked miserable, collapsed into himself. I offered paltry comforts without knowing whether they had any basis in reality, assuring them that everything was going to be all right, then wearily dragged myself home to catch a couple of hours' sleep.

Later that first day we were told that my mother appeared to be out of immediate danger but that it was too soon to say whether she'd suffered brain damage, too soon to say how or even whether she'd revive. We were plunged then into a timeless limbo, feeling alternately numb and tender from moment to moment. How long it lasted I can't now say with any certainty. On the afternoon of what I recall as the third day but which may have been only the second, she slowly opened her eyes and, smiling the sweetest of smiles, gazed gratefully at each of the four faces peering down by her bedside. There were my dad and David, who'd come down from Harvard where he was a freshman, Carolyn, and me. No doubt about it, she was thrilled to find herself alive. It was a precious instant, a warm helping of reaffirmation after so much cold fear. Suddenly we were all laughing and wiping our tears at the same time, thinking and probably now saying, "Everything's going to be all right."

Not immediately or easily but sooner than you might think, it was. That's to say, we all returned to the lives we'd been leading, trying hard not to look back. My dad cleared his calendar and, I suppose, consolidated his debts yet again to raise enough ready cash to take my mom on a five-week spin around France and Catalonia in a little gray Simca he arranged to purchase in Paris. After nearly twenty-seven years of marriage, it was to be the first time they'd traveled together in Europe, not to mention their first extended pleasure trip by themselves. The grand tour with which Carolyn and I had started married life the summer before seems, in a small way, to have inspired him, as he tried to give my mom some sense of still another new beginning for their marriage and herself. I can imagine her asking, "How come we never did that?" or me advocating travel as a panacea while she was convalescing. My dad kept a travel diary, making entries stop by stop. Striking for their opaqueness, they seem to follow the *Guide Bleu* in tone and content: vistas and meals are uniformly superb. The only anecdotes that don't seem canned involve cross-cultural set-tos with a hotel manager in Paris who accused them of stealing a towel and a French truck driver who disapproved of a passing maneuver my dad had executed as they crossed the Pyrenees. Only in the fourth week is there a hint of anything personal. On a rainy and overcast July 31 in Geneva, they marked my Mom's forty-seventh birthday by staying in their hotel room till four-thirty in the afternoon "enjoying a wonderful day of relaxation—even Scrabble in the daytime! . . . in ways that count the very best day of our trip."

In that same time, Carolyn and I had gone even farther, to what was literally the other side of the inhabited world. I'd won a Fulbright fellowship to Southeast Asia for which I'd applied without credentials or purpose, except to get as far away as I possibly could and have what I dreamed would be a life-shaping adventure. I was twenty-three, Carolyn twenty, and we'd been married for a year when we flew off to Tokyo and Hong Kong, en route to our destination with no real idea of what to expect. Obviously, we'd married very young. It's less obvious for anyone born after 1950 that this was unremarkable in the fifties. Sex had already been invented but unlicensed cohabitation was still a decade or so away as the sort of thing that could be announced to a young woman's parents. If she and her young man wanted to wake up together as well as go to bed, they usually married. It was a state you could fall into without earnest discussions of your "relationship," your "terms," or your "lifestyle." With a heedlessness that's simply shocking in the light of today's elevated and ennobling standards, we improvised as we went along, just as we later became parents without any inculcation on "parenting." We were so heedless that we never got around to buying a sofa till Amy and Nita were on their way to college, by which time the poor waifs had been dragged through a dozen homes on four continents by parents who occasionally communicated in snippets of Hindi and atonal Burmese and Chinese, the way an earlier generation took refuge in Yiddish when they didn't want to be understood. We had a common language and history all our own that we'd have had to give up if we'd ever thought of giving up on each other, which, to my immense good fortune, we never did.

All this exists on another, more accessible memory loop, one that seldom needed untangling. The only plan we acknowledged to ourselves when we set out can easily be nailed in retrospect as a tricky and transparent attempt by me to rationalize my impulsiveness. At the time, however, it seemed an insight, worth making into a creed. That plan was to have no plan; we'd live in the present, we said. Back then we knew that matrimony was supposed to be a deep and serious business as well as a social hurdle we were required to jump. But the terms "wife" and "husband" came off our lips a little awkwardly at first. We didn't yet know a Chinese term that covered our deepest vows, the ones that hadn't been declared before a congregation. That term is 爱人 or *airen*. In the Maoist era, it usually referred to a wife or husband; earlier, to less formal arrangements. What the characters literally mean is "love person," which is what we felt we'd found in each other.

My parents landed in Paris just two months after my mom's release from the hospital in New York. By then we'd taken up residence at 615B Prome Road in Rangoon, then the capital of a multiparty democracy in what was still called Burma. It never would have occurred to me, in that dreamy time of discovery in what seemed a serene land, to draw a parallel between my mom's dash to New York, with its catastrophic aftermath, and our flight to Asia, which took us in a year's wanderings north to Mandalay; east into the Shan hills; later to Siem Reap in an idyllic Cambodia where carpet bombing and mass murder were nightmares yet undreamed; south to Moulmein; then west, setting off from Calcutta, into India's dust and turmoil, its minute-to-minute pageant. But now, looking back across our lifetimes, I realize how similar our impulses to cut loose really were. I was her son, except I wasn't fleeing from my mate and seldom looked back in that time, once I sensed that distance from my parents could be fortifying.

My parents' getaway to Europe may have bought a little time for their marriage, but it still unraveled. As their dissolution proceeded, it was not without its little ceremonial touches. Just as you might be asked to an engagement party, we were invited to Westport, where they rented a cottage for the summer of 1963, for what proved to be a disengagement lunch. As host and hostess, my parents treated us a bit formally, as if we were guests, not members of the family, seating and serving us at a picnic table with a view across an inlet that led to Long Island Sound. Then, over dessert, as our infant daughter nursed or napped, we were cheerfully informed that they had been apartment-hunting for my mom, who was about to move back to Manhattan, and that this would be the first step to a legal separation that would most probably lead to divorce.

Soon after our mother moved into her new East Side apartment, she wrote a letter to my brother David, who was then in south India, teaching at a Christian missionary college near what was still called Madras. In it, she tried to present her move back to New York as something other than an emotional breach—as a calm decision based on a logical recognition of differences—but her words fairly crackled with emotion: she felt "nausea" when she looked back at her complicity in the move to Cleveland; her five years there had been "excruciating satire"; our father might be "well suited" to his pastoral work, but her denial of "its validity goes much deeper than I could ever dare to explain to one of my own children." That denial, she now contended, was the essence of their incompatibility. All this was squeezed onto one international airmail form. She had nearly run out of space and her writing had gotten very small when she ended with greetings for the Jewish new year, which would mark her liberation from the duties of a rabbi's wife. "I will spend mine not shaking 1,500 hands and not smiling," she vowed. (Mom's letter also addressed the question of how this second residence would be financed: The sale of the Steinway would cover a year's rent.)

Nine months later, my parents took Carolyn and me out to dinner on our fifth anniversary, ostensibly to mark the occasion but also, as if offering a cautionary example, to announce that this was the last dinner the two of them would ever have together as a couple: the separation was final, a divorce only months away. It was hard to know what to say. "I'm sorry" wouldn't have been welcomed. "I'm not surprised" would have seemed unfeeling. "Mazel tov" would have sounded sarcastic. My guess is I mumbled another form of "Good luck," maybe *"Bonne chance,"* or simply gave my parents one of those blank stares that my dad, in particular, had always found disconcerting. I'd left behind my urge to intervene in their lives and tell them what they had to do at Mount Sinai Hospital several years earlier. Even though my mom's return to New York had complicated my efforts to keep a safe distance, my deepest response to the looming end of the marriage without which I would never have existed was not terribly deep. This play had already had too many acts and we were all tired. The only one who could be described as caught in the middle was my youngest brother, Michael. With a year still to go in high school, he'd now been living alone with our dad in Cleveland for a year.

Years later, I was astounded to hear my mother casually describe the events of the following few weeks as the time "when your father left me." Considering that she had initiated the separation by decamping from Cleveland and reestablishing herself in New York, that she had already been living there for ten months, and that they had agreed on divorce, this didn't seem a small example of how the logic of the heart shapes memory. I may have allowed myself to mention one or two mundane facts, in spite of my vow not to go clomping into the emotional sanctuaries she'd fashioned for herself. Only later, near the end of her life, did I start to appreciate her tolerance for contradiction, to allow myself to think: Very well then, she contradicts herself . . . she contains if not multitudes, certainly more than one authorized version of her life.

If nothing else had happened, the end of my parents' marriage would have seemed anticlimactic, a final untying by lawyers. But something else did happen. Without reference to any member of his family except Michael, my dad went to Mississippi to pay his dues in what was called the "freedom summer" of 1964. He would have gone anyway, I think, but at this moment he was at a turning point; to all appearances freer himself, in the sense of less attached, than he'd be at any other moment in his life. If I were using these events in a novel, it would be tempting to have his character ponder the example of Ben Goldstein and the Scottsboro case, as if he were proving a point or settling accounts. But as I've said, my dad wasn't one to brood on the past. I can't know, of course, but I don't believe he gave Ben a moment's thought as he traveled South in the second week in July. His own explanation was that he'd been moved to volunteer in a voter registration project by a more immediate outrage that no one could ignore: the abduction, disappearance, and presumed murder of three young civil rights workers—James Chaney, Andrew Goodman, and Michael Schwerner—outside the Neshoba County town of Philadelphia.

Even before that outrage, my dad had made himself conspicuous on the front lines of a civil rights struggle in Cleveland over school integration. He had called for the resignation of the school board; had served as a principal of a "Freedom School" during a one-day boycott by black students and their parents; had fired off a telegram challenging the mayor to give the movement's leaders a serious hearing; had taken a titular position with a mainly black group of ministers called the Emergency Committee of Clergymen for Civil

Rights. And regularly that winter and spring of 1964 in Friday night sermons more pointed and demanding than any he had delivered since barnstorming for Zionism two decades earlier, he had returned to the theme that Jews—specifically, the members of his congregation—carried weighty obligations in the cause of civil rights because, as he invariably reminded them in homiletic riffs on two of his most cherished biblical texts: *You know the heart of a stranger, for you were strangers in the land of Egypt;* and *You shall love him as yourself, for you were strangers in the land of Egypt.* The ethical imperative he found in Exodus 23:9 and Leviticus 19:34 was applied explicitly to such touchy matters as employment practices and property values. A Jewish businessman who was serious about his faith wouldn't be satisfied to deplore bigotry, wouldn't even be satisfied to be an equal opportunity employer; he would actively seek to recruit blacks and refuse to deal with real estate brokers or banks that discriminated; and not only that, he would take a lead in welcoming black families into the eastern suburbs of Shaker Heights and Beachwood to which Cleveland's Jews had fled from the central-city neighborhoods they had once inhabited. Here, reminding the members of his temple about their ethical obligations when they might be tempted to think of the equity they had in their homes, he was being deliberately provocative. His temple happened to be in Beachwood, outside the city limits; none of its members had children in the Cleveland public schools. His own son, they all knew, was in a private school in which Jews, let alone blacks, were hardly numerous. Yet here he was injecting himself with a preacher's zeal into an increasingly angry controversy over inner-city schools. Many members of the temple were roused and heartened by his sermons, but an undercurrent of grumbling began along with a trickle, then a flow, of anonymous hate mail, some from Jews.

"Your own temple ran more than once from the *schvartzes*," one of the letters said. "Your own congregation has no intention to practice what you preach." Another letter came with a clipping about a court case involving a slumlord with an obviously Jewish name. "How fortunate is the Negro to have Rabbi Arthur J. Lelyveld to carry the torch for the whole Negro race," it said, "while his people profit and get rich by offering them slum conditions at a surburban price. And yes, indeed, servile positions in their beautiful and distant houses."

Members of the temple board were aware of these undercurrents. Some of them were ready to blame the rabbi. "Why doesn't he stick to his Jewish knitting?" one wondered aloud. All that was *before* he answered a call from the National Council of Churches to go to Mississippi after the July 4 weekend in support of the young volunteers engaged in the voter registration drive in which James Chaney, Andrew Goodman, and Michael Schwerner had just sacrificed their lives.

My experiences on the following Friday amounted, metaphorically speaking, to a collision at an intersection, a pileup of various issues, public and personal, making for one of the densest, longest days of my life. That day started eventfully enough for me. As a freshman general assignment reporter in the newsroom of the *Times*, my task that morning was to go to Queens and check out a tip from Simon Wiesenthal, the renowned Nazi hunter in Vienna, that a notorious death camp guard and convicted war criminal was now living there under the name of Mrs. Ryan. If she was using her original Christian name, she would be known as Hermine Ryan. And if Wiesenthal, who had helped trace Adolf Eichmann to Buenos Aires, was right, she could be found in a blue-collar neighborhood called Maspeth. The assignment seemed to promise a day of tough sleuthing. Maspeth in that time contained a lot of Ryans. I made a list of all their addresses and started ringing doorbells. It wasn't so tough. I had to ring only two. When I asked the first Mrs. Ryan I encountered whether she knew of another who had come fairly recently from Austria, presumably with a German accent, she said that would be Russell Ryan's wife and directed me to an address on 72nd Street. There the door was opened by a tall, large-boned woman in short shorts striped pink and white, with a matching sleeveless blouse, her hair up in curlers; she was brandishing a paintbrush. The conversation at the threshold of the little house, as I've remembered it down through the years, went something like this:

"Mrs. Ryan, I need to ask about your time in Poland, at the Maidanek camp, during the war."

"Oh my God, I knew this would happen," the Maspeth housewife said, breaking into sobs. "You've come."

Now noticing that the quote doesn't appear in the article I subsequently wrote, I wonder if she actually said, "You've come," or I supplied the words when telling others that I was received by Mrs. Ryan in Maspeth as if she'd expected me. Not in print but in occasional recountings over the years, I may have forgotten the "as if." In any event, mine was the finger of fate and it was I who had to listen, as we sat in her tidy living room with its Alpine scenes and cuckoo clock, to her weepy, self-pitying narrative of how she'd never been anything but a lowly guard, with no authority or choice, who anyway had spent most of her time at the death camp in the infirmary.

When I got back to the newsroom, an editor I knew slightly stopped by my desk with a sad, strangely deferential expression on his face. "I was sorry to hear about your father," he said, speaking softly. Inevitably, I heard condolence in his words and saw it in his face. The man realized I had no idea what he was talking about and started backing off. I had to pursue him, seize his arm, and practically shake him to get him to tell me that my dad had been hospitalized in Mississippi after being attacked near the town of Hattiesburg by a couple of local whites. After that frightening overture, I heard the blunt facts with relief. At least he was alive.

Some thirty years later I opened a survey form from the town of Hattiesburg, Mississippi, that had been mailed to newspaper editors across the country. *Have you ever heard of Hattiesburg, Mississippi?* the first question asked. I checked "yes." *If yes, in what context?* it continued. "My father was beaten there with a tire iron in the summer of 1964," I wrote.

He'd been in Mississippi for four days, in Hattiesburg for three. The movement had assigned him two tasks. One was to reach out to the Jewish community in Hattiesburg as part of a broader attempt to soften local resistance to the struggle for black rights; the other, to go door to door on backstreets where blacks lived to encourage residents to seek to register to vote despite all the hurdles white registrars could be relied upon to throw in their path—the patronizing questions and intimidating stares, the tricky forms and tests on which any trivial error would be grounds for instant disqualification (never noticed, of course, in the case of whites). He got precisely nowhere with Hattiesburg's Jews. There was no rabbi resident in the town that July, and the two former presidents of the congregation he managed to contact were not inclined to be helpful, fending him off with what can only be called white lies; they didn't know, they said, the names of the current officers. The synagogue itself was locked. "The Divine Presence," he later said, "was not at home."

In the black community, it was everywhere, he felt. The three hours he spent canvassing prospective black voters that Friday morning had been especially encouraging. He and the white college student he'd been accompanying then turned their steps to a black Baptist church where a lunch of fried chicken and black-eyed peas awaited the canvassers. On the way, as he later explained to two FBI agents who took his statement, they ran into two black high school girls who'd been canvassing on another street with a white college student. So now there were three white men and two black girls walking together past the Hattiesburg stockyard at lunchtime. It was a provocation, they soon learned, as a bunch of white kids started taunting them with cries of "nigger lover" and "white nig-ger." One of the students then suggested they take a shortcut by turning down a railway track that ran in the direction of the Baptist church. They'd gone about a hundred yards when a cream-colored pickup truck, with no license plate, barreled to a screeching stop at the foot of the embankment that carried the track. Two large white men jumped down from the truck and charged up the slope, cursing "nigger lovers" as they came. The younger, bigger one carried a tire iron. In that instant, my dad would tell his congregation in his first sermon after Mississippi, he thought of Ionesco's play *Rhinoceros*. "I thought of men being converted into rhinoceroses, and this was the way they charged us."

The girls ran; the other two volunteers remembered their train-ing in nonviolent resistance and moved away in opposite directions so as not to give their assailants a bunched target. They then ducked their heads, pulled their knees up, and rolled over to shield their most vulnerable organs. My dad had been through a training session himself in Memphis at the start of the week but two impulses got in the way of his training. One was to put himself between the on-rushing men and the girls; the other was to speak to the attackers. It all happened in seconds and he hadn't yet got a word out when the tire iron came cracking down on his head, leaving a deep gash on his brow, just missing his right eye. It came down again, on the back of his skull, then the young attacker moved off to bash one of the stu-dents while the other guy took his turn, kicking and pummeling my dad where he'd fallen, leaving him dazed but able to walk with the sup-port of the two students. They turned down the first street they came to, with the pickup truck again in pursuit, accelerating toward them as if to run them down. Once they had jumped aside, the men were in the street again, brandishing the tire iron and an aluminum pump.

The blood from my dad's head wounds had soaked through his shirt by the time they finally reached the church. From there he was taken to the Methodist Hospital. By then the story of the assault and his picture were out on the wires. Telegrams poured into the hospital. He used the backs of some of the telegrams to draft a statement on the assault. One that arrived later, I now discover, was from my mom. HORRIFIED BY NEWS AND WORRIED, it said. SHALL I MEET YOU IN CLEVELAND OR WHERE LOVE TOBY.

That afternoon I managed to get through to my dad in the hospital in Hattiesburg. From a medical point of view, he'd been lucky. He'd lost a lot of blood and had needed some stitches on his brow, but he'd escaped brain damage and, as far as the local physician could determine, a concussion. The plan was to keep him overnight for rest and observation and release him the next day. Having established that much, I returned to the case of Hermine Ryan, née Braunsteiner, the Maidanek guard in whose living room I'd sat that morning in Maspeth.

I scurried up to the editorial library of the *Times* to see what I could learn about Maidanek, a camp that stood in plain view on the outskirts of Lublin, a major city in eastern Poland. The gas chambers and furnaces went into operation there toward the end of 1942 and continued belching smoke until the Red Army drew near in 1944. As many as 360,000 persons had been killed there, the majority Jews (mostly Polish but also German, French, and Dutch). When the wind was right, the stench drifted toward town. That was the overview. Looking for anecdotal testimony on atrocities, I picked up a volume called *The Black Book*. In the early sixties, the field of Holocaust studies was not the industry it subsequently became; the word "Holocaust" itself was just coming into vogue as a term referring uniquely to the fate of Europe's Jews under the Nazis. But I didn't have to dig deep to find Mrs. Ryan. An SS guard named Hermine Braunsteiner figured prominently in the testimony of Mai-

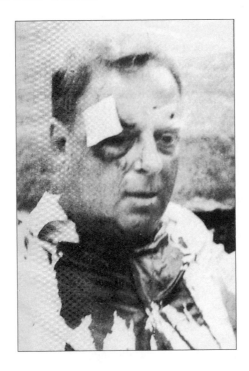

danek survivors. Those accounts gave the lie to her own self-portrait of a hapless young conscript convalescing in the infirmary. She was one of a small number of female SS guards at Maidanek who'd been charged with acts of extreme cruelty, even by the ferocious standards of the place. They selected inmates for the gas chambers on whims of their own. They took part in killings. "I myself saw babies taken from their mothers and killed before their eyes," said a witness quoted in *The Black Book*. Mrs. Ryan, called Braunstein there rather than Braunsteiner, turned up on the same page. No single crime was ascribed to her, but she headed the list of wardresses responsible for "unparalleled atrocities."

The testimony of the survivors commanded credence, even if I hadn't spoken to any myself. Novice that I was, it didn't occur to me that I might take more than one day on the assignment and find some. It didn't occur to my editors either; the operating assumption of newspaper reporting in that era was that most stories could be done in a day. I bolstered my account of my discovery of a Nazi death camp guard in Maspeth with a few paragraphs of appalling, graphic description drawn from *The Black Book*. That was enough to get it chosen for the front page. Then, as I was finishing up, my phone rang. The call was from Russell Ryan, the electrician who'd met Hermine Braunsteiner in Vienna, then brought her to America as his wife, enabling her to become a citizen. He'd never heard of Maidanek. He'd known nothing of his wife's wartime experiences, he said. But now, having just heard her version, he struggled to sound emphatic and manly, to banish any doubt from his voice. "My wife, sir, wouldn't hurt a fly," he said. "There's no more decent person on this earth." He succeeded only in sounding pathetic. He had never heard before that evening that his wife had been convicted as a war criminal in 1946 and had served a brief term in prison—for activities at Ravensbrück, not Maidanek—and could now face deportation for failing to acknowledge as much in her immigration papers. At that moment, I felt for him. Every word out of his mouth showed how dimly he understood his predicament. "Didn't they ever hear the expression 'Let the dead rest'?" he asked.

I'd have been totally offended if anyone had suggested to me that evening that I'd been thrown off-balance emotionally by the assault on my father and that I was now too overwrought to think clearly. At this distance, when I suggest it to myself, I'm unable to reach a conclusion. All I know is what I did. I went to the night city editor and said I was bothered that I'd not had time to attempt to verify the most hideous of the allegations against the death camp guards or draw a firm connection between any particular act of gruesomeness and Mrs. Ryan. We wouldn't, I said, treat anyone except a Nazi that way. A discussion then followed with a lawyer who said there was no way a Nazi could win a libel case in New York. That hadn't been my point but it led to further discussion with the news editor, who, sensing the uncertainty of an inexperienced reporter, decided to knock the story off the front page. As a way of showing it had not buckled under to that decision, the metro desk then decided to hold the story out of the paper so as to be able to get it "fronted" another day. Nevertheless, it ran on an inside page several days later, on my day off, shorn of the paragraphs I thought needed strengthening. The following morning I got a dressing-down from the new metro editor, Abe Rosenthal, who was to become the dominant figure at the *Times* for nearly two decades. With an insistance that could easily be mistaken for fury, Abe said something like this: "If I get a story of yours on the front page, don't you ever again go behind my back to get it taken off."

Looking back now from my own perspective as a former editor, I have to admit Abe had a point.

But all that—my search that morning for the death camp guard, the decision on deadline not to run the story, even the beating of my dad in Mississippi—proved to be prelude. The climax of that long and long-ago July day didn't really occur for me till I got back to our tiny walk-up apartment on Second Avenue with its nearly elegant glass doors and sloping parquet floor tilting down toward a huge sooty terrace out back. I've a distinct memory of my mother as she looked that evening, which is very peculiar because I'm all but certain that I didn't see her then. What I remember, I now imagine, is probably the picture I formed in my mind of how she must have looked when we spoke on the phone. I knew the expression she wore when she was avid with a single wish and need, next to which all other considerations suddenly became trivial: she looked taut, slightly flushed, and uneasy to the point of seeming brittle, as if she were anticipating that she'd be unable to cope with contradiction. That was the mood I must have heard in her disembodied voice when I returned her urgent call as soon as I got home.

She'd been galvanized by the news from Hattiesburg. Suddenly all her plans and decisions of the preceding months were cast aside. Just three weeks earlier we'd been told that we'd never see my parents together again as a couple. Now she was stepping forward as my dad's wife. She wanted to rush to his hospital bedside in Mississippi, not just as a gesture of loyalty to what had been but in full-scale resumption of a marriage that had already been consigned to lawyers for its last rites. I was to be the arbitrator and fixer, the go-between. All she wanted was for me to inform my dad that she was ready to come back and see to the logistics of their reunion. She'd leave for Mississippi on the next plane.

I'd taken the end of their marriage more or less in stride. The idea of its resumption was something else; it left me with a vague foreboding. The idea of its resumption through my own good offices felt regressive and wrong; not only did it contradict my distancing program, it gave me a faint physical sensation somewhere in the vicinity of my sinuses, as if I were approaching a psychic limit and might shut down. But I'd forsworn arguing with my mother, so I put through the call to Hattiesburg. No long conversation was needed once I broached my mom's plan. My dad said flatly that he didn't want her there; it was too late. He had been planning to tell me later, but now was the time: there was "someone else." He'd had all afternoon and evening in the hospital to make his plans. He'd arranged to be picked up by one of my Alabama uncles after U.S. marshals escorted him out of Mississippi. That would give him an opportunity to explain the situation to my mother's parents, who'd recently taken up residence close to her sisters in the Muscle Shoals area; in effect, to say goodbye. It was up to me, he said, to deal with my mother. I might have replied, "Why me?" but thinking of my dad in the hospital with a bandaged head, I didn't. I felt happy for my dad and sorry for myself. It was a handoff I hadn't foreseen.

It had to be to this sequence of calls that my mom was referring when, years later, she spoke of the time "when your father left me." She hadn't foreseen it, either, although she'd done almost everything imaginable to secure her separate existence. My dad had been so predictable, so long-suffering, she hadn't realized that he might reach a limit, too.

I said whatever I had to say to my mother that evening. I retain no memory of the conversation but always assumed that I'd found a way to deliver the message that there was no going back on her decision to end the marriage. Now I realize that I may have ducked that task, may have told her no more than that she wasn't wanted in Mississippi. Or maybe, after all, I told her more, but not bluntly enough for her to take it all in; maybe I omitted the part about "someone else." (The next day, she couldn't resist a final attempt to breach his silence; under the circumstances, it was a gesture approaching supplication: her telegram to my dad in the hospital, offering to join him in Cleveland, was sent early Saturday afternoon, almost certainly too late to reach him before he left for Alabama under federal guard. So it must have been forwarded to Cleveland. By the time it would have reached him there, she'd have long since gotten the complete message via her sisters in Alabama.)

Even after I'd spoken to my dad and then my mother on Friday night, that long day wasn't over. The muse of satire was lurking in the wings. We were not yet asleep when, well past midnight, the phone rang. Cursing and lurching out of bed, I bolted the five or six strides it took to get to the phone at the other end of the shallow apartment. There, standing naked at my desk in the dark, I was greeted by a hearty voice that identified itself as belonging to a reporter on night rewrite at the *New York Journal-American*, the Hearst flagship. The voice said that as a reporter myself, I would understand the need for the call. Talk about coming full circle. The *Journal-American* was planning to build its Saturday front page around the picture of the rabbi in his blood-soaked shirt (a strong news photo the *Times* fastidiously hadn't used, as if doing so might have created a conflict of interest for the paper where his son's byline was now appearing regularly). The rewrite man hoped to get something exclusive from that same rabbi's son. I begged off, saying I hadn't even known my dad was in Mississippi and had only talked to him since the attack about his injuries and family matters.

Staunchly refusing to acknowledge that our professional bond was already fraying, the hearty voice went on in words close to these: "Well, let me ask you this. Did he know what he was in for, what the risks were, when he walked into that den of lions?"

I exploded, saying that I wasn't going to stand around at one in the morning trying to answer pointless questions that answered themselves; that my father knew the country, read the papers, wasn't naïve, and, of course, had an idea of what the risks might be, of the sort of things that could happen in Mississippi. I was going back to bed, I said, and hung up with a bang, satisfied that I'd deprived the rewrite man of his story. On the newsstand the next morning, a deep picture of my dad in extremis dominated the *Journal-American*'s front page, under the lead headline which cried out in larger than usual type:

THE BEATEN RABBI:
RACISTS DID THIS

In early editions, a smaller headline on the front encapsulated the rewrite man's exclusive and his art:

He Knew What the Risk Was, Says Son

Later I was demoted to an inside page to make room for fresh exclusives; by the final edition, I'd vanished but the beaten rabbi continued to dominate page one, only the two lines of the big head had been reversed in order to freshen the page. They now said:

RACISTS DID THIS:
THE BEATEN RABBI

A crowd of 250 whites and blacks turned out at the airport to welcome my dad back to Cleveland as a hero. Services in the middle of July were always sparsely attended but there was an overflow congregation at his temple the following Friday evening when he spoke about his experience in Mississippi. Yet just two and a half weeks later, what's called the pulpit committee voted 12–3 not to renew his contract.

When the *Cleveland Press* broke the story on its front page, it was assured that my dad's activities on the civil rights front had nothing to do with the decision. Veiled allusions were then made to his strained domestic situation and the fact that he was now flagrantly keeping company with a woman not his wife without having announced any intention to seek a divorce. I suspect there may have been other resentments, including the time the rabbi spent out of town and his complaining about his salary, but these never got aired. Of course, the pulpit committee didn't want a rabbi to speak *against* civil rights; it just wanted, or so I now infer, someone quieter than my dad had been that spring and summer, someone who would confine his preaching to the sanctuary and not do battle in the wider community or beyond. Whatever moved the committee, its horrendously poor timing ensured its defeat. The temple's board was soon swamped with letters hailing the rabbi for his courage and demanding that he be retained. To arm his supporters, my dad had his secretary tally the letters and cards he'd gotten in the three weeks after the Hattiesburg assault. Out of 533—about half from Cleveland, half from the rest of the country—only 31 had been negative.

One of those came from a member of Benjy Schultz's congregation in the Mississippi town of Clarksdale who said my dad owed Mississippi Jews "an open letter of apology," having made life harder for them while making headlines for himself. The Clarksdale man then signed off with a crumb of fortune-cookie wisdom: "When one puts his head in a noose, he is bound to get rope burns." As far as I've been able to determine, neither Rabbi Schultz nor any of the other Mississippi rabbis found an occasion to say anything, at least where they might be heard, about what had happened in Hattiesburg to their colleague from Cleveland.

At the end of August, despite a rising tide of scandal-mongering about his marital situation and plans, a divided temple board reversed the pulpit committee and retained my Dad on what amounted to sufferance, offering him a mere one-year contract. In Hattiesburg, meanwhile, Clifton Keys and his nephew Kilmer Estes Keys, two citizens of rural Covington County who had been in town for the Friday cattle auction at the Hub City Stockyards, were arraigned on charges of assault and fined $500 each.

Again, if this were a novel trying to get inside its characters, I'd feel compelled to supply my dad and myself with clear motives. But these often turn out to be untraceable in our lives as we happened to live them. Just as I'd have been tempted to have my fictional dad spar with the shade of Ben Goldstein as he headed South, it should be even more obvious and tempting to have my dad's example looming over me when I made my own trip to Mississippi several months later. He'd been in the state only five days, but thanks to the mindless criminality of his assailants, that was long enough for him to live through a pivotal episode in his own life's narrative. With the beating in Hattiesburg, he went from being a clergyman who voiced concern to a clergyman who'd shed blood for a cause in which he believed, who'd actually been part of "the struggle." At that moment, it became a sure thing that it would be thought appropriate and necessary thirty-two years later to have "We Shall Overcome" sung at his own funeral. In that summer of 1964, when the bodies of the slain civil rights workers were finally retrieved from an earthen dam outside the town of Philadelphia, he became an obvious choice, not only as a friend of the family but as a wounded Mississippi veteran himself, to deliver a eulogy at Andrew Goodman's service. Never did he speak more feelingly, more purely:

> Not one of these young people who are walking the streets of Hattiesburg or Camden or Laurel or Gulfport or Greenville, not one of them, and certainly neither Andy nor James nor Michael, would have us in resentment and vindictiveness add to the store of hatred in the world. They pledged themselves in the way of nonviolence. They learned how to receive blows, not how to inflict them . . . To assume the risk so knowingly and willingly is to rise above all that is craven, sordid, limiting.

That was fresh testimony. It would have moved me had I been there to hear it. But I was working that day and didn't read the full eulogy until later. I spent much of that summer covering a less inspiring struggle, a series of riots that burned through the poorest black neighborhoods in a string of northern cities: first Harlem, then Rochester and Jersey City, and finally Philadelphia. The dominant racial stories in the country that summer were white violence in the South, black violence in the North. In a sense, they commented on each other. If their looting and burning carried any message at all, some underclass blacks in the North were saying, "What about us?" Racist whites in the South could say, "Look at that. Look to your own backyard." Landmark civil rights laws had just come into force, outlawing segregation and guaranteeing the vote, but they promised little to northern blacks. Suddenly it became obvious that the North would be a racial cauldron, too.

The riots that summer were my initiation in covering big breaking news. In Harlem I ran through the streets until the early hours of the morning on the fringe of the mob, stopping at a pay phone every half hour or so to read my notes to a rewrite man back at the office. On Lenox Avenue, late in the afternoon, I looked up to see a dozen or so bottles suspended in midair. I jumped into a postal van a second or two before they started shattering on the spot where I'd just been. The photographer walking with me was less fortunate. A bottle caught him in the face, fracturing an eye socket. In Rochester I was assigned to write the lead story but got so absorbed in seeing at first hand what was actually going on in the streets that I blew a deadline. I was then sidelined into writing features, sketches from the riot scenes rather than the rolling hard-news epics needed for the front page. By the time I was sent to Philadelphia, I'd been deemed trustworthy again. I'd learned how to balance the reporting and writing; how to be a team player; when to be in the streets, when to be writing; how to navigate and think my way through turmoil to shape a report that didn't just fling facts at random but tried to answer the question "What's really going on here?" In Philadelphia I felt I was coming of age as a general assignment reporter after barely seven months on the job. So when Lewis Bergman, the editor of *The New York Times Magazine*, asked me a couple of months later whether I had a story in mind that I wanted to do, I didn't think of my dad's example or the Mississippi "freedom summer." Instead, I thought of the north Philadelphia ghetto and the racial politics of the City of Brotherly Love. "As a matter of fact," I replied, "there's something I'd like to do in Philadelphia."

Without pausing to ask about my idea, Bergman walked off to huddle with other editors while I continued to correct galleys of a piece I'd done on Vassar College. When he returned, he said something like this: "OK, we've talked it over. You can go to Mississippi." Only when he was leaving the paper, about ten years later, did I tell him that I'd meant Pennsylvania.

That's just a newspaper anecdote, of course. It's bereft of the kind of deeper motive you might want to give a character in a novel. It assigns too large a role to chance. It makes life a tissue of happenstance. I'd reinvent it if I weren't seeking to avoid reinvention here. As matters stand, I'm left with the simple fact that I never set out to follow my dad. I just swallowed hard, grabbed the best assignment going, and went to Mississippi.

On my first or second night there, I found myself in a black church in Meridian where nineteen white men from Philadelphia, including the sheriff and deputy sheriff, were scheduled to be arraigned the next morning on federal conspiracy charges. They were accused of conspiring to deprive James Chaney, Andy Goodman, and Michael Schwerner of their civil rights by murdering them. Chaney's mother spoke with passion, delivering a testimony from deep within herself on justice and her conviction that her son had not died in vain. Then everyone in the church except two men in blazers crossed arms and joined hands to sing "We Shall Overcome." The network reporters, the wire service reporters, the *Time* magazine correspondent, and other newspaper reporters were all holding hands and singing. Having the idea that reporters weren't supposed to show their feelings or take sides, I was one of the abstainers. It was an uncomfortable moment. I wondered if the other abstainer was an FBI man. He turned out to be John Herbers, a *New York Times* reporter I'd yet to meet. Standing aside like that, it might have occurred to me that as a professional bystander, I'd chosen a very different vocation from my dad's, a different way of engaging the world.

It might have but probably didn't. If I had a father figure to bear in mind in connection with the Philadelphia, Mississippi, assignment, it wasn't my own father. As I was leaving for the South, more than one editor in the newsroom made sure I understood that the executive editor of *The New York Times*, Turner Catledge, actually hailed from the town of Philadelphia. This was offered as a word to the wise, but what the warning was supposed to convey I never found out. I'd talked to Mr. Catledge only once. After noticing a story I'd done, he'd called me to his office to get to know me and, in an offhand, pleasant manner, to ask about my ambitions. I said I wanted to be a foreign correspondent, preferably in Asia. I believed it was his doing when, a short time later, I was summoned to the foreign desk and—happenstance intervening again—offered the Congo: not my first choice, not the wisest place to go with two infant daughters, but an early start nonetheless on the correspondent's career I'd dreamed of. My next destination after Mississippi was to be Africa.

I spent a miserable day and a long miserable night in a Meridian motel room after five or six days of reporting in Philadelphia, failing to find a theme on which I could thread my impressions. With each passing hour, I felt increasingly desperate; half my time went to pushing down the irrepressible thought that this assignment was proving to be beyond me, that Mr. Catledge was about to discover how overrated his newest foreign correspondent really was. Then an obvious theme that had been staring me in the face made its way into my consciousness. I would write about the social stratum that thought of itself as making up Philadelphia, Mississippi's "responsible majority." They may have been neither responsible nor a majority but that's how they saw themselves. Loosely defined, it was the stratum that embraced the country club members who lived in the best houses; those who filled the churches on Sunday; and any others left over who despised the idea of racial integration but couldn't afford resistance, who never joined the Klan and wouldn't have been asked—all of whom now seethed with resentment because the whole country associated their town with a lynching. The truth, I would write, was that the town never had any doubt about where to look for the leaders of the conspiracy. The sheriff's office in the Neshoba County Courthouse was the obvious place to start. But the "responsible majority" had remained silent. We're talking here, of course, exclusively of whites. Some were silent out of fear; most viewed the three murdered men as intruders and didn't see anything wrong with confronting intruders. "How can it be murder?" one citizen asked. "They agitated it."

It didn't occur to me that I was writing about the people in town with whom Turner Catledge had grown up, the people there he knew best. When the time came to check the galleys, an editor on the magazine took me aside and told me that he wasn't supposed to say anything but it was in my own interest to know that the executive editor had read the piece and wasn't happy with its tenor or theme. He thought it overdrawn and ridden with the sort of stereotypes people like me foisted on the South. But Mr. Catledge had raised only one specific issue. In my account of an interview with the hospital administrator, a man he had known, I quoted this pillar of the community as using the word "nigger" three times. Probably, Mr. Catledge had said, the man had said "nigrah" and my Yankee ear had failed to catch the subtle difference. With a self-restraint that's not always a hallmark of powerful editors, he asked that I be challenged on that point alone without being told who'd raised the question.

I said this hadn't been my first trip to the South, that I was aware of the usage "nigrah" but "nigger" was what I thought I'd heard, what I'd written in my notebook. Now that I'd been challenged, I had to acknowledge that I was less than 100 percent certain of my ground, maybe only 95 percent. I said we could drop the quote but I didn't see any basis for changing it. The man at the magazine who'd given me the heads-up took an agnostic position on whether I'd do best to bend before the instinct of the native son who happened to be our leader. He left the choice up to me. I said I didn't want to drop the quote.

I heard nothing from Mr. Catledge about the article when it appeared; it was a silence that reverberated some in my mind. He'd been copied, I knew, on a mild letter of complaint that I'd received from one of his hometown's leading citizens. The leading citizen had told me he'd been too preoccupied with running his timber business to pay much heed to the execution of three civil rights workers or the furor that resulted. I quoted him at length to his distinct disadvantage; he helped clinch my case that the "responsible majority" had reacted to the murders as if they had no possible bearing on the community that gave rise to them. From the office of the executive editor came a polite message saying Mr. Catledge trusted I'd replied and, if I didn't mind, would like to know what I'd said. Later, after I'd been in the Congo for a couple of months, I finally heard from the executive editor himself. His letter seems to have survived only in my memory; as it's fixed there, Turner Catledge wrote that he'd reread my piece after his first visit to his hometown in some years. People he trusted there had vouched for its accuracy and told him it had helped to unfreeze discussion of large, unavoidable issues. He wanted me to know that he was now proud of my article.

I crossed paths with Turner Catledge a couple of times in later years when he cruised through the newsroom on visits to New York after retiring to a genteel life in the Garden District of New Orleans. "Greetings, from your friends in Philadelphia, Mississippi!" he called out on the first of those encounters. By then he may have forgotten that he'd sent me on my way as a foreign correspondent. The article he'd deplored was now our bond.

No new bond was formed between my dad and me by our limited experiences in Mississippi in the same fraught and uplifting time. That shouldn't be surprising. Our relationship as father and son had been jelling for twenty-seven years by the time he went to Hattiesburg. I hope I found an occasion to tell him that I'd thought his eulogy for Andy Goodman very fine. Almost certainly he'd have said something to me about my article on the town of Philadelphia. But appearing as it did a couple of Sundays after his divorce and remarriage, when he had just moved into a new household and taken on a new family, it wasn't something he could have been expected to dwell on. I saw him once before I left for Africa and then not again for a year and a half. Mississippi didn't turn out to be an experience we consciously or retrospectively shared; it would be truer to say it was when we diverged, as sometimes happens with fathers and sons.

7

DRAMAMINE

My dad traveled more widely in the last decade of his life than he had in all of the first seven, serving as a shipboard chaplain with luxury cruise lines for weeks and even months at a time. The postcards in his assured hand arrived with their bland, affectionate greetings from places I never expected to see as well as places where I'd hung out as a foreign correspondent. Bali and Bora-Bora, Bombay and Cape Town, the Galápagos and Panama, Istanbul and Odessa. It was a curious reversal of our accustomed situations: I was deskbound in New York; he was out roaming the world.

I doubt it has anything to do with his cruises and postcards, but a nautical image sticks in my mind when I try to characterize our relationship in these years. The image is in black and white and the look of the vessel is definitely retro, as if it sailed in from a screwball comedy like *The Lady Eve* or *A Night at the Opera*, my dad's all-time favorite movie. The ship is maybe thirty yards from the pier. It is coming, or going. The turbines have either just shut down or they're about to churn; the gangplank is about to descend or be stowed. My dad is at the rail, smiling amiably and waving. I wave back. It's a metaphor in the form of a daydream; just as the ship neither sails nor docks, so we never quarreled and seldom got close. Thanks to our unusual Dutch name, when we cropped up in each other's lives, it was not infrequently in a remote thirdhand way: I'd be asked whether I was any relation to the rabbi; he'd be questioned as to his connection with me. Such queries should always have drawn a prompt, emphatic answer, but sometimes that didn't happen. Occasionally we both displayed a tendency to fence with our questioners as if they were prying.

"He's the father of my grandchildren," my dad would sometimes say. Later on, his response to the question of whether we were related became more cryptic. "Yes," he'd say, "but only through marriage." He got a kick out of seeing how long it took people to solve the riddle; I missed a beat the first time myself, but his pleasure in these exchanges was so obvioiusly good-natured that I resisted the impulse to ask whether he thought he'd divorced me along with my mom.

In my own case, I was sometimes oversensitive about what questions on my relationship to the rabbi might imply. If the person seemed to know who Arthur Lelyveld actually was, I was normally proud to be his son. But once I became an editor, I started to imagine that I could hear traces of a Jewish folk belief, on which I too had been raised, that *The New York Times* was full of "self-hating Jews." If I caught a whiff of that, a suggestion that a settling of Oedipal scores might be tied into my involvement in the newspaper's coverage of the Middle East, I'd get huffy and combative in defense of the paper's integrity. As an editor, I'd now and then find myself on the wrong side of a reporter's notebook. Then the question might come from journalists writing about the *Times* and having, in the current mode of reporting on the media, to dwell more on the personalities and supposed auras of editors than on the content of their papers or the work of talented writers they recruited—an approach that easily led them to wonder why the *Times*'s editor was not a more engrossing or newsworthy character. The fact that he was a "rabbi's son" could be presented as an explanation, as if all rabbis and their sons were cut from the same drab cloth, and I could hardly complain. It's an absolutely just and potentially redemptive punishment to make an editor feel what it's like to be on the receiving end of coverage.

When it came to encountering a portrayal of myself that left me feeling all bent out of shape, nothing compared to an occasion, much earlier, on which I'd found myself stripped of my status as a layman and presented as a seeker after ontological truth. A piece I'd written about the "watermen" of Chesapeake Bay—the gatherers of its crabs and oysters—was included in an anthology designed for undergraduate writing courses as an example of "two rhethorical modes." (I couldn't have told you so myself, but these were said to be "analogy and symbol.") Even by present-day academic standards, the editors who researched my background were a little careless. "Joseph Lelyveld is a distinguished rabbi," they wrote. "His writings deal with religion and what is happening to religion in society today . . . In this essay, Lelyveld draws an analogy between the larger subject of human existence and life on a small spot of land on Chesapeake Bay." That was supposed to be me, if not in a nutshell, then on the half shell. My little story about lives on the bay—made possible by crustaceans and bivalves outlawed as *trayf* under Jewish dietary rules—had been turned into a rabbinic allegory.

Looking back, I'm struck by the care my dad and I seemed to take to avoid talking about our working lives or issues that interested us both. At one point, while he was president of the Central Conference of American Rabbis, I engaged in a heated correspondence with the organization's executive director, a rabbi in full cry who accused the *Times* of using its news columns with malice aforethought to undermine Israel. I told my dad about the exchange and may even have sent him copies. He either smiled or sighed—a tic passed from generation to generation, known in the family as the Lelyveld sigh—but offered no comment. He understood that the approaches of an advocate and a journalist had to differ. I wouldn't say that our conversational detours were designed to avoid disagreements because

I'm not aware that we did disagree; if anything, they were designed to avoid any possibility of disagreement, to keep our limited encounters mellow and positive.

Kidding, another family reflex, was still acceptable, but only within circumscribed limits. I sensed that I overstepped them a little during another of his presidencies; this time, of the American Jewish Congress. It was the late sixties and I was living in New Delhi, covering India and Pakistan. A British colleague showed me a small item on the front page of a London paper that said my dad had called on American Jews to boycott France and French products, not excluding Bordeaux and Brie, to protest President de Gaulle's refusal to sell replacement parts for French military equipment to Israel. Given my dad's history as a pacifist, I thought he'd opened himself up for a spoof. I then had a small inspiration. It occurred to me that I could use two airline boarding passes I'd saved as bookmarks after a recent trip to Pakistan. I'd rushed there to cover the fall of a military strongman, catching the first available plane, which happened to be a Saudi Arabian Airlines flight crammed with Hadj pilgrims. I'd returned on Lufthansa. So I took the Saudi and German boarding cards and sent them to my dad with a note saying it had taken some doing to uphold his boycott and avoid Air France. He didn't kid back as I might have expected. He disclaimed responsibility for the statement; then, I imagine, he sighed. As the years passed I came to realize that it was now possible to ruffle his dignity as it had not been when we all were younger. He wanted the respect that was due him, especially from his sons. Not realizing that it had ever been in question, I may have been slow to catch on.

Since my mother had reestablished herself in New York and remained single, I eventually found myself more involved with her, especially when she had one of the several health crises of her later years. It was not an involvement I always accepted gracefully. I wanted to do the right, the dutiful, thing, but having concluded that I needed to keep a safe distance from my parents, I tended to do it grumpily, relying on Carolyn to provide the grace. Early on I even staged a psychodrama to show myself—my mother too—how challenged I'd become in the department of filial devotion.

It was a seemingly serene Sunday morning in July, in the townhouse we were temporarily inhabiting off the King's Road in London. I was still at the breakfast table reading the book review pages in the Sunday papers. A couple of months earlier, the apartheid regime in South Africa had honored me with an expulsion order. Now we were enjoying a civilized, pain-free interlude at the epicenter of what was called swinging London, awaiting reassignment. My mom, who had just moved in for a visit of a week or two, approached the table with a coffeepot and asked whether I'd like my cup refilled. Her voice seemed to upend the room, causing it to spin. I fell off the chair and felt for a moment as though I were going to slide down the incline that our parlor had suddenly become. Finally I crawled to a couch where I diagnosed myself with a brain tumor.

After a second dizzy spell a day or two later, I went to see the National Health Service physician to whom our family had been assigned. The doctor examined me, found my reflexes and muscle control in order, then asked whether I was experiencing any strains in my marriage. None whatsoever, I replied, taking immediate umbrage at the suggestion that my trouble could be emotional. He persisted. Was there a new factor in the household? I professed to be puzzled by the question. A visitor perhaps?

"Just my mother," I said.

I don't recall the doctor actually saying "Aha." He didn't need to; his raised eyebrows and a slight tip of his chin said it anyway. He then made a commonsense suggestion. Instead of offering me a prolonged course of psychotherapy, courtesy of the British people, he said I might consider taking Dramamine, the seasickness remedy, whenever I expected I'd be spending time with my parents. It was a little embarrassing for someone who, at twenty-nine, was supposed to be an adult, but I sailed through the next few months on Dramamine, until my new assignment to India came through. By the time my mom visited us in New Delhi a couple of years later, I'd used up or mislaid the tablets but found I could manage without them.

I now understood that there were unresolved matters left over from my childhood—"issues," they call them—but I resolved not to open the box. I'd have said then that I didn't want to stop my life to look back; that for better or worse—more likely, better *and* worse— I was who I was going to be. At thirty-two, I copied into a little notebook something Albert Camus had written in his notebook when he was that age: "At thirty, a man should have himself well in hand, know the exact number of his defects and qualities . . . be what he is. And above all accept these things." I might not have had myself well in hand, the defects might have outnumbered the qualities—I certainly hadn't written *L'Etranger*—but still, I thought, I could accept these things. Really, I would have argued, was there any choice? I was now living some approximation of the life I meant to live, and that, as far as I was concerned, was what mattered, so long as I could avoid getting sidelined into a newspaper job for which I could muster no passion. I was so busy charting my own peculiar vocational course, dodging good assignments for which others might have killed, that I had no emotional energy to spare for bygone loose ends, even when I suspected they were not exactly gone.

It was Michael, my youngest brother, who eventually broke through my defenses, challenging after a protracted siege my settled view of what had happened in our family when I was growing up. Michael had no reason to poke into my buried history of thwarted yearnings and unexpressed resentments; he had a historical inquiry all his own. When I first heard of it secondhand through our middle brother, David, I was haughtily dismissive. What Michael had gradually come to suspect and then believe was that our father wasn't, in fact, a biological party to his birth. Michael's revisionism so contradicted my memories I could only conclude that he was indulging an unhealthy—which is to say sick—fantasy. What was really a little sick was my absolute unwillingness to take in what I was hearing. After all, I was supposed to be the open-minded reporter, ever ready to pounce on life's surprises. Instead, I reacted like an official spokesperson for an entity that no longer existed except in memory—the family in which we'd grown up.

Instantly I remembered the breakfast at Penn Station at the end of the summer of 1947 when our parents, as joyful together as I would ever see them, told David and me that we'd soon have a little brother or sister. I remembered my proud and beaming dad coming down the hill six months later on a balmy evening in late February with the news that the baby was a boy. I remembered how that baby was cherished and how I used his arrival to beat down my doubts and questions about the durability of our family; forgive the sacrilege, but the holy infant gave me a sustaining faith. Now, when that infant was a college graduate, our parents were unequivocally sundered, and I had a family of my own, I still felt a need to fight for that faith. Otherwise I too might have had to ponder what had really gone on in those years, which was exactly what I'd resolved not to do. So even as I approached middle age, I kept my hands over my ears like the hear-no-evil monkey, until the facts were implicit no longer; and even then, I didn't want to listen.

What had started for Michael as speculation, based on extravagant gifts he received every year on his birthday from a surprising source, as an interpretation of broad hints our mother dropped in later years when he came to New York, and as irrefutable inference, from the image he would see when he looked in the mirror, was explicitly confirmed for him by our mom just before she was about to undergo a potentially dangerous operation on her obstructed carotid artery when Michael was thirty-one (and I was all of forty-two): genetically, if not empirically or emotionally, he was the son of the suave Renaissance scholar and man of the theater, Maurice Valency— "V" from my mom's first summer as a graduate student, Val from the days when we got to know him as a family friend.

Michael's distinct and eventful story would be worth a serious telling if he were ever moved to write it. I left for college when he was six and we never again lived in the same place for more than a couple of weeks at a time, so I didn't live through it. My purpose here is something else; it's to wonder about my strange midlife reaction to his scoop. My adamant resistance to a fact that obviously affected him far more than me finally gave way, but now I was equally adamant about the conclusions I drew. I was angry rather than curious; in my own mind, I'd been the victim of a con. It seemed obvious that the careful assortment of warm memories to which I'd clung as a child had now been torn to shreds, revealed to have been nothing more than a tissue of illusion and wish fulfillment. My issue wasn't the sanctity of marriage; it was discovering how fragile my sense of my world had really been, how much it had depended on a story line that now seemed to have intersected with reality only now and then.

As for my mom, my attitude toward her became even more problematic than when I'd assaulted our parlor floor in London with my head. Old images popped up, clamoring for reinterpretation. I could remember my mom, for instance, fuming in the summer of 1948, the year of Michael's birth, about my dad's supposed flirtation with a woman in his office. It was easy now to read that as a diversionary tactic, whatever the unknowable facts. And, inevitably, I had to ask myself how, later on, she could have brought Val into our family circle and set my dad up to be his pal, or left Michael in Cleveland with my dad when she split for New York. What was really going on in those situations? How did she understand them? It was as if she'd been the director of a drama of which only she had the script, the

rest of us merely improvising parts she'd assigned. My seething was softened only by distance, for once again I was living in Africa; it hadn't, I realized, been the healthiest reaction I could have had. At this late date, it was depressing to see how little I'd surmounted these ancient contingencies and unhealed wounds from my youth; many others, I assumed, resolved such matters sooner with less gritting of the teeth. Still, as always, I clung to my long-standing slogan about getting on with life. More than ever, that was what I felt I had to do.

What I did not even consider doing, then or later, was to talk to my mother about this chapter in her history. My interest in contemplating that reality, her reality, plummeted from zero to a frigid minus. Several times she opened the door to such a conversation, but invariably it was by dangling some once juicy tidbit about my dad that I didn't need or want to hear. It had always seemed a matter of basic etiquette that I not become a bearer of old or fresh gossip between my parents once they were talking only through lawyers. Yet there was more to my stiff resistance than etiquette. I felt I was protecting myself from a knowledge of old grievances I'd neither be able to judge nor purge from my mind.

So more years passed before I managed to touch on the siring of my brother while talking to my dad. By then I think I'd heard from one of my brothers that the only part of Michael's discovery that had really surprised our father had been the identity of the other man in that long-ago triangle. While he'd never surrendered his sense of himself as Michael's real father, the true paternal presence in his youngest son's life, he'd suspected for many years that he hadn't done the actual fathering. At some point, suspicion became knowledge only, it seems, to be promptly and fiercely repressed. He hadn't allowed himself the obvious thought that Valency might easily have been the other man, even though Val had been the cause of a passing jealous pique when my dad had first heard of him, five years before Michael was born.

Here the plot thickens. We were taking a stroll from his apartment near Shaker Square on a golden autumn Saturday, at a point when I'd already turned fifty and my dad was well on his way to eighty. He spoke without recrimination. It was as if he were simply musing about a surprising discovery some researcher had made in a field that had once been of intense interest to him. The discovery seemed to carry less of an emotional charge for him than it did for me, which strikes me now as not quite but nearly understandable, since the question was still fairly fresh for me but roughly forty years old for him. Indeed, he sounded almost disinterested when he remarked, "I always thought it was Henry Monsky."

This would have been a little startling if I hadn't resolved never to be startled by my parents again. Monsky, an Omaha lawyer and family friend, had become a national Jewish figure as president of B'nai Brith, then a growing and vigorous movement in communities across the country. I'm not sure I ever saw him again after we left Omaha, but I could remember my distraught mother coming into the room I was still sharing with David on Riverside Drive one night when my dad was on the road in the spring of 1947 to shake me out of my sleep, on the upper bunk of our double bunk bed. I was only ten but she needed to talk to someone about Monsky's sudden death from a heart attack. I was a little surprised then that she was so upset. Even now I can't begin to draw any conclusions from her reaction. But I've finally done the arithmetic my father must have done: Henry Monsky's fatal attack came nearly eight months before Michael was born. So it was not impossible.

But since we now knew that Monsky was not the right answer to the question that eventually hovered over Michael's parentage, I'm left wondering, as I didn't at the time of our stroll down Shaker Boulevard, how and when my dad settled on him as a suspect. Was it a supposition based on Henry Monsky's dark hair, liquid brown eyes, and brooding physiognomy? Or had my mom, deliberately or carelessly, scattered false clues? It's in this connection that the letter my dad wrote her on the plane to Pittsburgh exactly a week after my bar mitzvah now seems pivotal. If in the course of their stormy confrontation that Saturday back in that spring of 1950 she'd asked what made him so sure he was really his youngest son's father, it would have been easier for him to resolve to hold his family together if he could make himself believe that his rival had been dead three years than if he'd concluded Michael's biological father was actually living nearby.

But that confrontation was more than two years after Michael's birth. Which means that my recollection of my beaming father coming down the hill that balmy evening with the news of my brother's arrival was in no way an illusion planted by a con. And my parents' joy at Penn Station at the end of the previous summer had also not been feigned, even if there was a question that had yet to be answered in the back of my mom's mind. Gradually it dawned on me, while my parents were still alive and long before I ever contemplated this journey into my past, that I didn't need to dismiss all my happier memories just because the context had proved to be a good deal more complicated than I'd allowed myself to imagine when I was growing up, or later. It dawned on me because I found my mother dwelling with fondness on the time of our childhood, organizing her pictures and even more her memories, both of which she regularly ran through when I visited in her last years. Increasingly what came across in these renditions was a rekindled tenderness for my dad, from whom she'd heard nothing since their last alimony fight. Years before she had burned up the phone lines to Cleveland to collect gossip about his new marriage, but now when she got up the nerve to ask about him, it seemed she wanted to hear only that he was well; more particularly, I sensed, that he was well and sometimes asked after her. Since this seldom happened, I couldn't easily supply the answer she wanted to the question she hadn't dared to ask.

   She had long since moved back into the same apartment house
on Riverside Drive where we'd grown up and now spent hours staring at the familiar view across the Hudson. When she moved back,
I assumed it was to be near Valency, who had moved with his wife,
Janet, from our building to an apartment across the street. But it was
also to be in the place where she had raised three sons with my dad.
Eventually I realized that if this might seem contradictory to me, it
didn't to her. The frailer she got, the more she clung to life, and the
more she seemed to embrace the life she'd led, the same life she had
several times tried to abandon when she was in what might might
have been construed as her prime. In a tortuous, overpacked, almost
Jamesian sentence, she found words for her acute preoccupation
with herself in a letter she sent to David when he was going through
a difficult time, urging him not to procrastinate on life's big choices.
She had, she said, "spent a lifetime in delayed response, slow learning and now [find myself] finally living out the deep irony of belated

self-assurance but still dragging with me the old baggage of daily assessment of inherited values—my capacity for growth entirely wasted, or at least frustrated, as I think back over the ways I failed all of you as I floundered to protect myself from real or imagined pain and as I now find myself, treasuring an abstraction we call love with absolutely no sure way to express it."

Even before I managed to work out their meaning, I found those words lacerating when I read them for the first time, six years after her death. Each phrase is reasonably clear in itself, but once the phrases are strung together, she seems to be facing in two directions. The way I read it, at least, both her tendency to solipsism and her desperate love for her family are on display. Offering herself as a negative example to her middle son, she seems to be saying she should have broken out sooner and found her own way. At the same time, she's full of remorse over the fallout from her various failed attempts to do precisely that. I'm not sure whom she's actually talking about when she says she has "absolutely no sure way" to express her love; I'm not even sure she knew. I suppose it's for all the men in her life, including her sons. But I'm left with a feeling that I failed her; that in addition to being an attentive and dutiful son, I could have learned to be more accepting of the love she couldn't easily express.

When my mother was nearly eighty-one, our daughter Nita was married at our country place. For my mom, it was her first big outing since a terrible fall the year before; the day following her return from a cruise on the Baltic and tour of St. Petersburg she'd sustained brain damage so severe when her head struck the sidewalk on Broadway that she'd had to be hospitalized for more than two months. She'd recovered her ability to do the crossword puzzle in the *Times* before breakfast but now could no longer walk unaided. Our friend Arnold Beichman, who often said she was the most beautiful woman he'd known in his college years, wept when he saw how frail she'd become; moved by the care she had taken over her dress and appearance after all she'd been through, I thought she still looked beautiful. I could tell that she was in a high state of anticipation—to see Nita as a bride, to be sure, but also, and perhaps even more, to get a glimpse of my dad, who had come with Teela, his wife, and my stepsister Robin. My mother didn't remark afterward on his failure to greet her or to otherwise acknowledge her presence in the course of a long June afternoon in which they were often at fairly close quarters. I sensed that she was devastated. I understood the awkwardness of the situation for him, but knowing how much it would have meant to her, I felt disappointed, too.

The next and final family gathering at which they would both be present came only six months later. It was near Boston at the bar mitzvah of Michael's son, Victor. My dad, who'd flown in from Cleveland with his wife, said a blessing for his grandson. Midway through the luncheon reception that followed, I went off to make a phone call, probably to check in with the news desk in New York. The path of my return brought me near the restrooms. My mom, who was a little stronger than she'd been six months earlier, was slowly making her way in that direction. So, I saw, was my dad. Realizing they were about to converge, I stopped in my tracks to watch what happened as their aging bladders brought them together. I don't know if I had the thought at that instant but it was obvious that this encounter, twenty-nine years after they'd divorced, was likely to be their last.

When their paths finally crossed, my dad beamed his warmest beam. My mom's face lit up with sheer delight. The conversation couldn't have lasted more than a minute. My dad stood there holding both my mother's hands and told her how glad he was to see her. She said how glad she was to see him. He asked about her health, she asked about his; they both said they were fine. Then, having expressed mutual pride in their grandson, they wished each other well, kissed, and parted. For my dad, it was what it was, a warm greeting, the sort of thing he could always be relied on to carry off persuasively, even on the way to the men's room. For my mom, I've no doubt, it was the end of their story, the simple resolution for which she'd been longing, a sign that he could still look on her with affection and that therefore she had a right to her fond memories.

Never again did I hear her mention him in an anxious voice. Never again did she offer to tell me how he'd wronged her. When I had to tell her, two years later, that he'd been diagnosed with an incurable brain tumor, she shook her head sadly and her eyes welled with tears but she asked no questions. The reaction was just as inward and muted when, five months later, she had to be told that he'd died. In considering the end of his life, I knew, she was contemplating the end of her own. Frail as she was, she outlived him by nineteen months.

If there is such a thing as an easy and gentle death, then both my parents had easy and gentle deaths, in that their consciousness of what was happening to them had been unplugged weeks before the end. Their final days were not so easy, however, for those who came to their bedsides. In each case, we had the unnerving experience of being stared at with an absolute absence of recognition, comprehension, or curiosity; when it came to evoking interest or feeling, we were undifferentiated from the chairs on which we sat or the paint on the walls.

My dad's mind receded gradually as if on a dimmer. In the early weeks, there were intriguing moments in which it was impossible to gauge his level of understanding, to tell whether the absence of any trace of anxiety reflected a profound acceptance of what he might have called God's will or a surrender of the neurons that carry feeling. He said nothing and showed no reaction beyond a slight raising of his eyebrows when I had to tell him, in the waiting room of a neurosurgeon we had just consulted at the Cleveland Clinic, that the doctor had advised that all we could do was try to keep him comfortable. I wasn't sure that he had taken in the significance of what I'd said until a couple of hours later when over lunch he suddenly broke his silence. The sages had always taught, he said, that how many days you had left was less important than how you lived them. Then he seemed to drift off. I couldn't tell whether he had been cogitating all that time, or if a failing synapse had just fired. A few weeks later, when he had been moved to a hospice, Teela, trying to draw him out of his enveloping silence, gamely asked what he was thinking about.

"I'm thinking about how everything goes down the chute," he said.

"What does that mean?" she said.

My dad wasn't ready or able to venture into rabbinic dialogue. "I don't know yet," he said irritably. "I'm waiting to find out."

To lighten the moment, I kidded him for perhaps the final time. "A theme for a sermon," I said. "Rabbi Lelyveld will preach on 'How Everything Goes Down the Chute.'" He looked at me blankly.

On my next visit, someone asked whether he was comfortable. By that time anything he said was likely to be composed mainly of words that had just been spoken to him, as if he had nowhere else to turn for vocabulary. "I'm afraid I'm comfortable," he replied. That was either a fortuitous fusing of language or the last word on what it's like to wait for the end in a hospice. It was also among the final sentences he uttered.

Inevitably, his funeral was a large public event, marking his thirty-eight years in Cleveland, where I had never lived. The sanctuary seemed to be almost as full as on a high holy day. Sitting a dozen feet from his casket, braced by Carolyn, Amy, and Nita, I half closed my eyes to find a private space for my grief as the eulogists variously characterized his contributions to the congregation, the wider community (including the Jesuit university where he had taught a course on Jewish values in his last years), and his place among the leaders of Reform Judaism. I don't think I was summoning any particular reaction from my murky depths, but one popped up that caught me entirely by surprise. Suddenly I imagined a little boy with curly blond hair, a projection from pictures taken when I was three or four, running up a slight slope, through high grass, on a summery day. The little boy was calling, "Daddy, Daddy, Daddy . . ." I've no idea whether there was a trace of memory in that scene imagined by the fifty-nine-year-old executive I'd somehow become. But I knew at once, as the service ran on and the little boy kept calling, that it was a feeling I'd suppressed practically all my life.

My obsessive mother had nearly everything about her own end figured out. A decade before she died I started receiving letters detailing who would get which stick of furniture and insisting that she be spared medical measures that would sustain her in a state in which she was less than herself intellectually or emotionally. She divided up her trove of family photos into three parts, one for each son, and emptied her file cabinet, discarding her research notes for a book on the history of actresses, their social standing and accomplishments, that she had never managed to write in the years she was teaching at Columbia and Juilliard. She also sent me a suggestion as to how we might dispose of her remains.

She was in the hospital when her exhausted cardiovascular system shut down whole areas of her brain, leaving her in what appeared to be a vegetative state. Soon it became impossible to feed her with a spoon. Her physician, arguing that she might still revive, arranged for her to have a port inserted in her midsection for feeding purposes. The question of when we should enforce the wishes she had duly expressed in all the necessary documents and affidavits was upon us. It was answered by the hospital, which wanted her moved to a nursing home. Instead, we arranged to have a hospital bed placed in her living room.

On an impulse similar to the one that leads some parents to play Mozart for infants, I kept operatic arias and serene choral music playing on a boom box, hoping the music would ease whatever was left of her spirit. As the sun set on an early winter Sunday, three days after we brought her home, we were into Haydn, specifically the soprano's aria in the first part of *The Creation*. The lyric may celebrate fruition, all the world's fragrance and beauty, but the piercing melody wouldn't be out of place in a requiem. The aria also seemed reverentially suited to the roseate light show taking place on the New Jersey Palisades as I sat at my mother's bedside, holding her hand. I'd yet to turn on any lamps, so the light in the room was fading; in this gathering dusk, I was feeling mellow and contemplative as I cast my mind over random moments of her life. Then, without warning, I heard the faint gurgle in her throat heralding her departure. Her passive grip tightened as a shudder ran down the length of her body. Before I could move or tell my wife in the next room what had happened, she all of a sudden existed only in memory. I grieved for her, for myself, for all of us. Once again, when it was too late to say so, I felt I loved a parent of mine unreservedly.

The only thing for which she had left no instructions was a funeral or memorial service, so we improvised one in my own Riverside Drive apartment as the sun started to set a few days later. It was at the other extreme from the public event in Cleveland the previous year. One of my mother's sisters and some of my Alabama cousins were there; so were two of the nursing aides who'd cared for my mom in her final years. In all, there were fewer than two dozen people sitting in a circle. Her sons said what they wanted and needed to say. Carolyn read a poem she had written. Then I played Haydn's glorious hymn to the beauty and balm of a trackless Eden, the brand-new, God-given world. Finally, my brothers recited the Kaddish, the prayer for the dead, while I moved my lips, pretending to lip-synch the mainly Aramaic, not Hebrew, words, which, shamefully, I'd never managed to master.

If I could have made myself believe that my mother might have been watching, I'd have felt that her critical spirit would have approved of the ritual we'd devised. I didn't believe, but I felt it anyway.

My mom's wistful idea for the disposal of her remains could have been inspired by a picture of an empty beach in an airline ad touting winter getaways. If her three sons wouldn't regard it as an imposition, she wrote, they might meet on a beach and scatter her ashes on the outgoing tide. It struck us that this was not something we could easily, or perhaps even legally, do in season on a beach where people swam. A sailboat might have suggested another approach but none of us was a sailor. In fact, none of us seemed eager to be tour director for this particular excursion, so the conversation languished, with the result that Mom's ashes were parked for some months in a cardboard canister in a closet. In the summer, as Carolyn and I were getting ready to leave for Maine, where we long ago had built a cabin on a stretch of remote coastal wilderness, I thought of the canister and announced to my brothers that they'd be welcome to participate, while we were there, in the consigning of our mother's ashes to the Bay of Fundy at high tide.

David couldn't make it but Michael did. So just before lunch on a brilliant midsummer day, we clambered down the rocky promontory in front of the cabin to a ledge about ten feet above a kind of flume where the water surges with a loud whoosh when the tide is in; there I pried the metal top off the canister. For a brief moment, we stared at the cinder and powder and tiny chips of bone to which our lovely mother had been reduced. Then, as if casting seeds, I sent maybe a third of the contents into the air over the glistening sunlit water.

In the solemn emotion of the moment, there was one practical detail to which I'd failed to pay heed. You guessed it—I'd neglected to notice which way the wind was blowing, and, of course, it was blowing our way. My brother and I stared at each other with mixed amazement and horror, followed, after a moment or two, by a splash of hilarity. A fair portion of Mom was now in our hair and eyebrows. She clung to our shirts and our skin.

Later, after dousing our heads, necks, and arms, we assured one another that she'd had a taste for metaphor and therefore might have appreciated this one. Our mother might even have repeated what her own mother would say whenever we failed to do what was asked, or did it wrong. Grandma B always said, "They meant well."

NOTES

1: MEMORY BOY

20 **wrath**: The prayer that shocked me so by its invocation of a vengeful God can be found in Jeremiah 10 and Psalm 79 as well as the Haggadah, the prayer book used at the seder. A close reading of the text makes clear that the condemnation of "the nations" is not nearly as sweeping as the unqualified opening line seems to make it. Vengeance is being sought only against those who have defined themselves as enemies by persecuting Jews, not against all non-Jews, for the prayer goes on to specify the "nations" that "have devoured Jacob . . . and laid waste his habitation." Nevertheless, the cry for vengeance once made many Jews in the West uncomfortable and it was often omitted. Only after the Holocaust did it come back into widespread use. In fact, the Bible is very specific about the obligations Jews have to non-Jews, "the stranger that is within thy gates." Deuteronomy 14:21 says he can be served food that Jews are barred from eating. Leviticus 19:34 goes further. "You shall love him as yourself," it says.

2: A GREAT DISAPPOINTMENT

40 **Horace Mann**: In 1943 the Boys' School of Horace Mann, an independent school, had long since migrated from the Columbia campus in Morningside Heights to the Riverdale section of the Bronx. My mother is probably referring to another portion of the school, left behind in Manhattan, that was coed and still tied in those days to Teachers College, where she had studied.

3: NOT FROM THIS PLACE

62 **Sulzberger:** One of my father's tasks as a Zionist official was to try to persuade the *Times* that it was giving the anti-Zionist position excessive coverage. He never got to meet the publisher but periodically called on Sulzberger's second-in-command, Julius Ochs Adler. Iphigene Sulzberger, who as the only child of Adolph Ochs was in a position to cast the decisive votes in favor of making her husband and son publishers of the *Times*, had a change of heart on the question of a Jewish state when the images of the Nazi death camps became fixed in her mind. "I began to contribute to the cause of establishing a State of Israel," she said in her memoir, *Iphigene*, written with the help of her granddaughter Susan Dryfoos (Dodd, Mead, 1981). Her husband remained anti-Zionist but the existence of a Jewish state was never an issue for their son, Arthur Ochs Sulzberger, or his son, the present publisher. The idea that the *Times* was untrustworthy on Israel hung on in parts of the Jewish community, however, despite the outstanding work over many years of a succession of fine correspondents. So it happened that a half century after my father's visits to the *Times* on behalf of the Zionist movement, representatives of Jewish groups who wanted to talk about the paper's coverage of Israel were usually steered to his son.

79 **Steve:** Wise's letter to my brother was subsequently included in a selection of his letters, *Stephen S. Wise: Servant of the People*, edited by Carl Herman Voss (Jewish Publication Society, 1969), under the heading "To Michael Stephen Lelyveld (19 days old)."

4: BEN

87 **reliable interest:** A scandal in another religious community involving clerics and boys moves me to add, though it shouldn't be necessary, that our play was entirely cerebral. I say this only to douse what may be inevitable suspicion. If we ever played a game together, it was Ping-Pong.

94 **Clayton and Sayre:** Yes, Zelda Fitzgerald was a Sayre. The third and current Temple Beth Or was built in 1952, just across the road from the Montgomery Country Club where Zelda met Scott and where the first Jew wasn't admitted until the mid-1990s. Joe Scott's used car lot now stands on the site of Ben's temple.

96 **culture or civilization:** This line of thought was hardly original with Ben. In 1925, the year before he was ordained, a survey of sixty-five Reform rab-

bis found fifty who said they were more comfortable with an interpretation that considered Judaism a "civilization" rather than a "cult." In part, they were expressing discontent with the content of Reform Judaism as it had evolved to that point. To some, it had come to seem theologically inadequate and spiritually barren. Such thinking culminated in 1934 in *Judaism as a Civilization*, a book by Mordecai Kaplan, the founder of what came to be known as Reconstructionist Judaism. In his own discourses on these themes, my dad came out for God. In his book *Atheism Is Dead* (World Publishing, 1968), he repeated a rabbinic joke: "Before Mordecai Kaplan says there is no God, he reverentially covers his head with a skullcap—since no pious Jew will utter God's name with uncovered head!"

103 **right of sharecroppers**: Nate Shaw, the pseudonymous narrator of *All God's Dangers*, Theodore Rosengarten's classic account of the life of a black sharecropper in this period, said it even more bluntly: "The nigger was disrecognized; the white man in this country had everything fixed and mapped out. Didn't allow no niggers to stand arm and arm together." Nate Shaw, whose real name was Ned Cobb, lived in Tallapoosa County and was jailed for more than ten years for his part in the events Ben and his friends wanted the governor to investigate.

120 **Paramount**: Much later the FBI turned Morros into a double agent, which became the basis for a memoir, *My Ten Years as a Counterspy*, and of course a movie, *Man on a String*, starring Ernest Borgnine. The relationship of Morros and Zubilin is laid out in *The Haunted Wood* (Random House, 1999) by Allen Weinstein and Alexander Vassiliev, who had access to KGB archives; at times, who was exploiting whom was less than clear from Moscow's point of view.

120 **played the piano**: The station chief's readiness to sit down at the piano fits the picture of him as a cultivated man that was drawn by Polish officers and intellectuals who survived their encounters with him in 1939 at Kozelsk near the Katyn Forest. He spoke fluent French and German as well as imperfect English and offered good tea, cigarettes, and conversation to those he was interrogating, sometimes even lending them books from his personal library, according to a description quoted by Herbert Romerstein and Eric Breindel in *The Venona Secrets* (Regnery, 2000).

122 **KGB**: Historians sometimes use the terms KGB and NKVD interchangeably when they discuss Soviet espionage in this period. Before foreign intelligence functions were concentrated in the KGB, the two overlapped for a time.

122 **Truman**: Evidence that President Truman was never briefed on the decoding of the Venona cables can be found in *Venona: Decoding Soviet Espionage in America* by John Earl Hynes and Harvey Klehr (Yale, 1999), page 15.

123 **Ben Franklin Club**: I've been unable to find documentary evidence outside Ben's FBI file of the existence of such a club. Indeed, Dorothy Healey, later the party's organizing secretary for Los Angeles and author of *California Red*, a memoir, told me that she'd never heard of it. However, there are other examples of branches of the party being named after founding fathers in the late thirties and during the war in order to bolster its bogus claim to being independent and rooted in American political traditions. Earl Browder, its leader, said it stood for "the complete amalgamation of Jefferson's teachings with those of Marx, Engel, Lenin and Stalin" (see *The Heyday of American Communism* by Harvey Klehr [Basic Books, 1984], page 211). Ben's episodic membership in the party seems amply documented, in any case. The FBI even had the numbers of his party membership books.

5: POSSIBLY INVOLVED

132 **another on Spain**: Gannes's coauthor on *Spain in Revolt* (1936) was listed as Theodore Repard. After he left the party, Theodore Draper stopped spelling his name backward. It then appeared on such pioneering studies as *The Roots of American Communism* (1957) and *American Communism and Soviet Russia* (1960).

132 **one of the eleven**: Gil Green was Harry Gannes's brother-in-law and the party leader in Illinois. At the command of the top echelon, which convinced itself that fascism was coming to America, he became a fugitive with orders to keep the party alive underground in the event of its being banned. Dodging the FBI for nearly five years was all he could manage, to judge from his memoir, *Cold War Fugitive* (International Publishers, 1984).

140 **linen handkerchiefs**: Kohlberg's name became synonymous with the epithet "reactionary" in liberal circles during the McCarthy era, a result partly of a suspicion that he was a front man for Chiang Kai-shek. It was never shown that he took foreign money, and in any case he was a more original and diverting character than epithets might suggest. In what he claimed was his 467th letter to *The New York Times* and the first ever published, he analyzed a boast by China's Communists that 530 million fruit trees had been planted in a small portion of the Yellow River delta. With considerable wit, Kohlberg showed that this would amount to more than a thousand fruit trees per acre. "In my native California," he wrote, "40 fruit trees per acre is more or less

standard procedure." The letter is quoted by William F. Buckley Jr. in an introduction to a sympathetic, politically one-sided biography of Kohlberg, *The China Lobby Man*, by Joseph C. Keeley (Arlington House, 1969).

144 Dear Ed: Hoover was a "great friend" of Niles, according to Peter Grose in *Israel in the Mind of America* (Knopf, 1984), where the White House aide is described as Hoover's "fellow Washington bachelor." According to Grose, Niles was unlucky in the one great love of his life. This was for Stephen Wise's daughter Justine. The infatuation that Niles then nursed as his "life's sadness" had something to do, in this interpretation, with his sympathy for the Zionist cause: through Justine, he fell under the influence of her father. It also seems likely that it was through the Wises that Niles first heard of Ben. "I've a recollection," he says in his letter to Hoover, "that this Rabbi Goldstein was a relative of the late Rabbi Stephen S. Wise."

145 Hoover: In his book *Venona: The Greatest Secret of the Cold War* (HarperCollins, 1999), Nigel West contends that military officials were reluctant to give the FBI director a clear picture of the secret work going on at Los Alamos.

146 party member in California: Its single reference to Ben's activities in New York had him as a member of a branch of a "listed" group called the International Workers Order, a fraternal organization with Communist ties. The memo didn't say whether he was an active member or when he had joined. It may have referred to nothing more than an IWO insurance policy, which is all that connected most of its members to the group. No mention was made of Ben's connection, starting as soon as he arrived in New York as a reborn rabbi, to the left wing of the kibbutz movement in Israel through an outfit called the Progressive Zionist League, which listed Ben as its organizing secretary.

153 publishing house: Farrar, Straus & Company, as it then was.

6: DEN OF LIONS

180 *The Black Book*: There were several distinct books by this name, mostly based on material collected after Soviet forces took over the areas where the death camps stood. This *Black Book*, subtitled *The Nazi Crime Against the Jewish People*, was published in New York in 1946.

182 had a point: Nine years later, Mrs. Ryan became the only person ever extradited from the United States to Germany on war crimes charges. According to witnesses, she had selected 1,700 inmates for gassing, including a couple of truckloads of children, had participated in the hanging of a young girl, and had whipped five women and a child to death with a lead-tipped whip. As it also turned out, she had risen to the post of vice-kommandant of the women's camp at Maidanek. According to Dorothy Rabinowitz in her book on Holocaust survivors in America, *New Lives* (1976), Russell Ryan not only stuck by her but learned to blame his wife's legal troubles on Jewish interests in the media. Starting with me, I suppose. In 1981, seventeen years after I rang her doorbell in Maspeth, Mrs. Ryan was sentenced to life imprisonment by a Düsseldorf court. In her fifteen years in prison, it was reported, she chose not to speak to other inmates. Her avocation was sewing dolls and soft toys. In 1996, after she had been found to be terminally ill with diabetes and gout—part of her left leg had been amputated—she was pardoned and released to a nursing home under Evangelical auspices in the Rhineland town of Bochum-Linden. Her husband was already living in the nursing home, awaiting her. She died there in early 1997. Russell Ryan of Maspeth, Queens, appears to have lived on in the nursing home in the Rhineland.

187 **Schultz:** Clarksdale made news of its own on the day of the attack on my dad in Hattiesburg: the town fathers removed all the chairs from the public library as their answer to the threat that blacks might attempt to integrate the place by sitting in them. There is no record that Rabbi Schultz had anything to say about that, either. But four years later, following the murder of Martin Luther King in nearby Memphis, he delivered the main address at a memorial service attended by 1,500 in Clarksdale's civic auditorium. "He did not fight persons, he fought evil," the rabbi said of the fallen leader, according to the report in the *Clarksdale Press-Register.* Several years later, near the end of his life, he sent a copy of that clipping to the American Jewish Archives in Cincinnati in hopes of leaving behind a redeeming example of his stance on racial issues. If he had opposed "Federal usurpation" in Mississippi, his covering letter said, it wasn't because he was "anti-Negro." It was simply "part of a philosophy."

7: DRAMAMINE
197 **small spot of land:** *The Perennial Reader*, edited by William Lutz and Harry Brent (Harper and Row, 1984).

PHOTOGRAPHS

Frontispiece: Arthur and Toby Lelyveld with their eldest (at that time, only) son, probably in the summer of 1940, possibly in Upper Michigan.

Page 10: Toby and Arthur at their commencement at Columbia University, 1933, seven months before they were wed.

Page 11: Toby in a publicity shot, about 1948, used mainly by the lecture bureau that arranged engagements for her to speak on *The Merchant of Venice,* or Jews in the theater, or the new season in the theater, or Jews in the new season in the theater, or other aspects of Jewish culture.

Page 18: Father and son, 1939 or 1940

Page 27: In Omaha, 1943, age five or six.

Page 35: The would-be actress posing and vamping for the camera in 1923 or 1924 when she would have been eleven or twelve.

Page 45: Elias Newman's watercolor portrait of Toby, late 1943 or early 1944.

Page 53: On the farm, 1943, between Lawrence and Layton Jensen. Courtesy of Betty Jensen Peterson.

Page 60 (top): Joe Lelyveld, my great-grandfather and namesake, in front of his cigar store at 1444 Madison Avenue, between 117th and 118th streets in Harlem, a couple of blocks from what was known as Mt. Morris Park, the center of a fancy white neighborhood at the time of the First World War when this picture was probably taken. The area later fell into decay but now many of the old brownstones have been restored. The park was renamed in 1973 in honor of Marcus Garvey, the black nationalist.

Page 60 (bottom): Joe Lelyveld; his son, Ed; and grandson, Arthur, around 1922 or 1923.

Page 72: Gift-wrapped for return to my parents in August 1945, at the home of yet another Joe Lelyveld, a Rockland, Massachusetts, podiatrist who was my grandfather's first cousin.

Page 83: On the Hudson River Dayliner, August 1948. Ben Lowell (formerly Ben Goldstein) appears between my brother David and me. Our mother is on the right.

Page 91: Margaret and Ben Goldstein at their wedding in 1926. James Waterman Wise, the best man, is on the right. Courtesy of Jo Rogers.

Page 92: Stephen S. Wise orating at a Liberty Bond rally on Wall Street during the First World War. (Bain News Service)

Page 113: After Alabama, Ben Goldstein at the Jersey Shore with Josie on his back, 1935 or 1936. Courtesy of Jo Rogers.

Page 153: Linda (left) and Josie Stern (formerly Linda and Josie Goldstein) with their father, Ben Lowell, at Josie's graduation from a Pennsylvania boarding school in 1948, about five months after Ben's ouster from Hillel and a couple of months before his departure for Havana. Courtesy of Jo Rogers.

Page 165: Toby Lelyveld posed with her dissertation, by Karsh of Ottawa.

Page 171: On the beach in Moulmein, Burma, in early 1961, steps from "the old Moulmein pagoda, lookin' lazy at the sea," which happens to be about seven hundred miles from Mandalay, where Kipling seems to put it in his poem of that name.

Page 180: Hattiesburg, Mississippi, July 10, 1964. (*U.P.I.* / *Corbis-Bettmann*)

Page 203 (top): Joe, Michael, David, and our dad in 1957 as David, then sixteen, is about to ship out as an unpaid "deck boy" on an Israeli freighter bound for Naples and Haifa.

Page 203 (bottom): Thirty-five years later, the same four at the bar mitzvah of Victor Lelyveld, Michael's son: Michael, David, and Joe with our dad, then eighty.

Page 207: Toby, in her late seventies, off on a cruise.

ACKNOWLEDGMENTS

In my eccentric, often whimsical quest for documents or records that might amplify or correct my memories, I incurred debts along the way to serious archivists and scholars. I'm grateful to Lyn Slome of the American Jewish Historical Society in New York where I delved into the papers of Rabbi Stephen S. Wise; Gary P. Zola at the American Jewish Archives in Cincinnati; Jane A. Avner of the Western Reserve Historical Society where the Arthur J. Lelyveld papers are housed; and Stuart Rockoff of the Goldring-Woldenberg Institute of Southern Jewish Life in Jackson, Mississippi. I also want to thank Micki Beth Stiller, a lawyer in Montgomery, Alabama, who has done her own research on the history of Temple Beth Or there, of which she is a member. I'm grateful as well to the congregation for the access I was granted to its archives. Rather than burden a personal narrative with the apparatus of scholarship, I'm sending a full set of the material I collected in various places on the life of Benjamin Goldstein, later Ben Lowell, to both the American Jewish Historical Society and the American Jewish Archives. Ben's nieces, Marion Bar-Din of Oakland, California, and Dorothy Lindheim of Berkeley, were helpful at the beginning of my quest in providing background on his family and the married name and probable locale of his one surviving daughter, Jo Rogers of Knoxville, who proved to be unfailingly generous and welcoming. The Wilson Library at the University of North Carolina at Chapel Hill granted permission for me to quote from the Olive Stone interview in the Southern Oral History Program Collection and to reproduce a handbill in the Howard Kester collection for a meeting in support of the Scottsboro defendants.

John Earl Haynes of the Library of Congress, a leading historian and demystifier of American Communism, pointed me to the tantalizing references to Ben Goldstein in a couple of the Venona decryptions, which are collated on the Web site of the National Security Agency; and Professor David Weiss Halivni, the distinguished Talmudist at Columbia University, guided me to an understanding of a prayer often said at the Passover seder that had been omitted from the liberal edition of the Haggadah on which I grew up. James Goodman, the author of a compelling narrative of the Scottsboro case, provided some valuable research tips.

My brothers, David Lelyveld and Michael Lelyveld, had the generosity of spirit to search their boxes of old letters and pictures, not to mention their memories, give my manuscript a close reading, and yet to accept my account as my account. Andrew Wylie's sympathetic and astute observations helped me conceive an approach to the material I write about here. Richard Eder, a treasured friend and colleague of long standing, was good enough to read a completed draft, and then helped keep alive the author's faith in his quixotic project when it was flickering. Jonathan Galassi, a great publisher and reader, did everything an editor can do to nurture a project into a book. Of course, none of these good people bear the slightest responsibility for any self-indulgence, willfulness, or blind spots that may be detected in these pages.